SWITZERLAND:
THE AWFUL TRUTH

SWITZERLAND:
THE AWFUL TRUTH

by Jean Ziegler

Translated from the French by
Rosemary Sheed Middleton

HARPER & ROW, PUBLISHERS
New York, Hagerstown, San Francisco, London

This book is dedicated to the memory of
Salvador Allende
Roger Genoud
Khariton Chavichvily

This work was first published in France under the title *Une Suisse au-dessus de Tout Soupçon*. ©Editions du Seuil, 1976.

FIRST U.S. EDITION

ISBN: 0-06-014799-7

LIBRARY OF CONGRESS CATALOG CARD NUMBER 77-11790

79   80   81   82   83   10   9   8   7   6   5   4   3   2   1

Contents

✓ Switzerland, or the Swiss Confederation: a republic in central Europe, originating from a pact made in 1921 among three Alpine valleys – Uri, Schwyz and Unterwald.

(*Larousse*)

✓ Its total land area is 41,295 square kilometres, i.e. 0.15 per cent of the earth's habitable land. Its population of 6,431,000 is less than 0.03 per cent of the population. The Helvetic Confederation is the world's leading market for money, gold and insurance; it is the world's third largest financial power, the eleventh industrial power and the home of the largest food processing industry. The Swiss are the second richest people in the world.

(Suisse, *OECD Economic Studies, Paris, 1975*)

Introduction

One thing I have learned and I know it in your stead
Dying myself:
How can I say it – there's something inside you
And it won't come out! What *do you know in your wisdom*
That has no consequences? . . .

Oh, goodness without consequences! Intentions in the dark!
I have changed nothing.
Swiftly vanishing without fear from this world
I say to you:
Take care that when you leave the world
You were not only good but are leaving
A good world!

Bertolt Brecht
Saint Joan of the Stockyards

History catches us wherever we are born. I was born in Switzerland. In *Les Rendez-vous manqués*, Régis Debray talks about the "summons of the imagination"[1] that draws together all the critical minds and revolutionary wills of a nation and an era into a single plan of action. I do not believe that any such "summons" exists today in Switzerland. Nor do I believe there is such a thing as History there, in the accepted sense of the word. To be precise, I think that the summons and the history are something residual and hesitant, present only in the mind, lived in the imagination by way of events elsewhere. My endeavour throughout this book is to bring them out into the open, to get them out from under the stifling and alienating blanket of fog which is produced by the ruling discourse and produces the silence and uniformity of consent.

For over a hundred and fifty years, a close-knit oligarchy that has never had a Vichy to cope with, and has therefore never been unmasked, has ruled a state and a people whose legislation, ideological system and bureaucratic machine are perfectly suited to its needs. Thanks to a monstrously hypertrophied banking system, as well as to the admirable institutions of banking secrecy and the numbered account, the Swiss oligarchy functions as a fence for the world capitalist system. With its daily takings it finances its own foreign ventures; Swiss multinational companies today control whole regions and populations – from Indonesia to South Africa, from Brazil to Guatemala. Switzerland is the only industrial state in Europe whose balance of trade with the poor nations is consistently in surplus. In the worldwide imperialist system, the banking barons of Geneva and Zürich also fulfil many other functions: they contributed to crushing Allende's Chile by first cutting down, then cutting off, its international sources of credit. They "stabilized" and then reinforced the racist dictatorships in South Africa and Rhodesia, and the totalitarian régimes in Bolivia and Indonesia. But the Swiss banking barons have won their most outstanding victory of all in the sphere of the ideological class struggle: by means of their superlative international propaganda machine and their corruption of large sectors of the political classes at home, they have managed to identify their strategy of pillage and receiving stolen goods with the national interest of the Swiss state and people. Speechifying incessantly about neutrality and peace, their faces half hidden by the flag of the Red Cross, the banking barons – cold monsters – succeed in persuading other nations as well as their own native subjects that they are philanthropists: rich, of course, but peace-loving and virtuous.

Why have I written this book? The worldwide imperialist system is "concrete absolute evil", in the Hegelian sense of the term. It dominates and ravages three-quarters of mankind today. I was born in the brain of the monster, at the "privileged" core of the system. I intend to fight it from there.

"Whatever is, is false," said Max Horkheimer. What is false in our world? In a rare moment of self-criticism Robert S. Mac-Namara, president of the World Bank and one of the major imperialist leaders, revealed the following figures:

> That half of the 2,000,000,000 people in the world who live in the underdeveloped countries suffer from hunger or malnutrition. Twenty to twenty-five per cent of their children die before the age of five. Of those that survive, thousands live an impoverished life because of brain damage, arrested growth or low vitality due to an inadequate diet. 800,000,000 are illiterate; despite foreseeable progress in education, there will be even more illiterates among their children . . . The average life-expectancy in the underdeveloped countries is twenty years less than in rich countries. One-third of the world's population (the industrial nations) has seven-eighths of the world's income, while the remaining two-thirds have to make do with the other eighth.[2]

As I say, there is only the faintest summons to be heard in Switzerland. I cannot claim to be the spokesman of a party, or a trade union or even of the Swiss workers' movement; I can only speak for a little-known fraction of that movement, on the basis of an ill-defined solidarity and will to unity, in the name of what I want that movement to be and to become. There is a Left, a workers' movement in Switzerland. But it has let itself be partly trapped in the fog of the consensus, of willing uniformity. I say partly, because its members still have some contradictory convictions, habits and rituals, and even occasionally an upsurge of contradictory activity. But, prisoners as they are of the models and values of the ruling class, they are reduced to taking one step at a time, for they have lost any total vision of what the revolutionary imagination is summoning them to.

In an earlier book, *Les Vivants et la Mort*,[3] I recounted my own odyssey. As a socialist parliamentarian and an academic theoretician, I am trying to fight a battle that is inseparably both theoretical and practical. This book is a result of that battle, and also a means of waging it. It is certainly not an overall sociological analysis of Switzerland. I would add – to forestall accusations of bad faith, though I fear I am wasting my time – that this book is not an attack on the institutional system (federalist, and comprising a variety of peoples, languages and cultures) brought into being by the Swiss over the course of six centuries of hard-fought history; it is not an attempt to assess the advantages of the system, nor is it concerned with making a sociological study of any aspects of Switzerland not directly connected with the understanding of the imperialist problem. Nor does it formulate a left political programme of any kind. Based on my personal experience, at home and abroad, it is a "sociography", so to speak, of the ruling capitalist class of Switzerland, of how that class operates today in its own country and in the world, how it is linked with the other imperialist oligarchies.

Our planet is a cemetery which the imperialist oligarchies are working to fill daily with more victims. I know one particular oligarchy extremely well, the one working from Switzerland. I want to show how it goes about its work. And at the same time, I want to show how this oligarchy makes Switzerland, as a nation and as a people, dependent on imperialism.

There is no doubt that imperialism, the highest stage of capitalism, is at present in "crisis".[4] But the "crisis" is one of reconstruction and adaptation, not of death. I can see at least two reasons for this:

1. Since decolonization, the hegemonic capital of the centre (that is, of the industrialized countries) has become more and more a worldwide phenomenon, and has thus effected a qualitative change in the social landscape of our planet. We are all familiar with Lenin's classic definition of the origins of the system of world domination and the practice of imperialism.[5] Since he formulated that theory, the major agent of imperialist aggression against the nations on the periphery (i.e. the Third World countries), the nature of the relationship of dependence it establishes in the three dependent continents, and its strategy of exploitation, have all changed. The chief aggressor against the poor nations today is no longer the capitalist state as conqueror, protector or trustee – as foreseen by Lenin – but a capitalist system that transcends state boundaries. This system operates without using – or at least not to the same extent as before – its former instrument, the state.[6] The specific social entity born of the change is the transnational or multinational company.[7]

The motive force of the multinational company is profit, and its social strategy is a continuing extension of its power over people and things. In the three dependent continents, as in the various countries at the centre, the multinational companies are tending to eliminate gradually the competition among themselves. (This is made definitely easier by the gradual abolition of competition among the various state systems. Peaceful coexistence between the USSR and the USA, to say nothing of the many mutual security agreements made between the two powers and their satellites, furthers the imperialist domination of many areas in the Third World. In other words, imperialism adopts certain rules for exercising its domination, and these rules reinforce that domination. This vital fact underlies the considerations that will emerge in my concluding chapter about the respective roles of the class struggle and the anti-imperialist struggle in Switzerland and in Europe.

2. Having sustained certain setbacks in their fight to keep control of raw materials – defeated in Cuba, Vietnam, Cambodia and China, and harassed by revolutionary forces (though these are still in a minority) in their own homelands – the imperialist oligarchies are today redeploying their forces. A number of questions need answering, in no particular order. In practical terms, what is the position of the international workers' movement today? On the chessboard of international relations, what is the policy of the socialist states and how great is their power? Inside the capitalist

powers at the centre, what positions have been won by the revolutionary forces? On the periphery, which are the bastions held by anti-imperialist forces, and which nations are achieving the material means to liberate themselves?[8] In theoretical terms, what positions have been won from the standpoint of the class struggle? And finally, what level has anti-imperialist consciousness reached at the periphery and at the centre?[9] I shall not of course be answering all these questions. But they underlie everything I write, and by analysing the case of Switzerland, I hope to contribute to finding some of the answers.

I make no claim – nor would I have the ability – to present a coherent and definitive theory of secondary imperialism, based on one man's analysis of one case. For at least two further reasons, this can be no more than a contribution. In the first place, secondary imperialism is caught up in the present crisis of primary imperialism, and is therefore in a state of flux; neither its new strategy nor the means available to it can yet be identified to any precise degree. In the second place, there is a strange invisibility about the activities of the secondary oligarchy. Given the absence of detailed statistics for investments and profits, the purposely vague or actually false reports given to shareholders, and the refusal of most senior management in such companies to answer enquiries, I am obliged to form my hypothesis on the basis of very inadequate information.

However, I have received invaluable help from four experts who have allowed me to use passages from their own recent work, giving statistics, dates of enquiries, and so on, with which to supplement or support my theoretical analyses. The extracts taken from Delia Castelnuovo-Frigessi come from "Colonialismo a domicilio: i lavoratori stranieri in Svizzera", *Il Ponte*, 1974, pp.1447-79. Those from Heinz Hollenstein are from "Die Entwicklungspolitik des schweizerischen Staates", in the review *Civitas*, vol. xxix, no. 1/2, October 1973, and no. 3, November 1973. Those from Beat Kappeler come from "Schweizerische Finanz und Dritte Welt"; and those from Rudolf H. Strahm come from "Schweizer Industriekapital und Dritte Welt": these last two are taken from *Schweizer Kapital und Dritte Welt*, published by Erklärung von Bern, Zürich. I would warn readers that at times, because of the context in which I quote them, these extracts suggest an interpretation which their authors would not fully accept. This is especially the case with the passages from Beat Kappeler, which have been slightly modified, and those from Heinz Hollenstein, which are not representative of his work in general. They are used essentially to illustrate my argument, and I make no claim to associate their authors with my conclusions.

I have also received much help from the reference department of the Federal Assembly in Berne, from colleagues in the United Nations Library and from the Institute of Development Studies in Geneva. I am especially grateful to Professor David Handley who agreed to read the English version of the manuscript and offered his helpful suggestions, and to Rosemary Sheed Middleton for her excellent translation of the book. And I owe a great debt of gratitude to Mme Micheline Bonnet for revising and tidying up my original text.

J.Z.

Notes to Introduction

1. Régis Debray, *Les Rendez-vous manqués,* Paris (Seuil), 1975, p.38.
2. Extracts from a speech given at the IMF Conference in Nairobi, 24 September 1973; see also P.Drouin, "Les chiffres de la honte", *Le Monde,* 5 October 1976, analysing the figures presented by MacNamara at the annual conference of the World Bank in Manila in 1976.
3. Paris (Seuil), 1975.
4. I borrow this phrase from Samir Amin, though without accepting all the theories on which his diagnosis is based, Cf. S. Amin *et al., La Crise de l'impérialisme,* Paris (Minuit), 1975. Several important authors have reached similar conclusions by way of different analyses: cf. especially J.Attali, *La parole et l'outil,* Paris (Presses Universitaires de France), 1975; A.Meister, *L'Inflation créatrice,* Paris (P.U.F.), 1975; C.Julien, *L'Empire américain,* Paris (Grasset). For an understanding of the original ideological sources and the origins of the praxis of primary imperialism, cf. H.U.Wehler, *Der Aufstieg des amerikanischen Imperialismus,* Göttingen, 1974. The studies collected by Wehler – himself heavily influenced by the Wisconsin school – and above all the pioneering work of Taylor, *The Tragedy of American Diplomacy,* 1959, cover the period 1865 to 1900.
5. See V.I.Lenin, *Imperialism, the Highest Stage of Capitalism.*
6. Of all the founding fathers of the sociology of imperialism, only Bukharin (in my view) clearly foresaw the development we are witnessing today – that is the development of capital as a worldwide system, the hegemonic cartelization of the banks, and the rise of the transnational companies that are supplanting the state and usurping its major economic and political powers. Cf. N.Bukharin, *World Economy and Imperialism.*
7. Cf. the United Nations Document no. ST/ECA/190, *Multinational Companies and World Development,* New York and Geneva, 1973.
8. There are two authors whose works seem to me indispensable to a knowledge of the struggles now taking place on the periphery: Roger Genoud and Régis Debray. Cf. R.Genoud, "Sur les révolutions partielles du Tiers Monde", *Temps modernes,* no. 328, Paris, 1973, pp.884ff; see also G.Delaprez, "Pour lire Roger Genoud", ibid., pp.876ff; M.Rodinson, "Révolution et révolutions, postface à Roger Genoud", ibid., pp.911ff. Cf. also Régis Debray, *A Critique of Arms,* vol. I and II (Penguin), 1977-8, and *Che's Guerilla War* (Penguin), 1975.
9. Jean Daniel expresses the antithesis of this question: "Since the world is changing faster than our wish to change it, where is the point of convergence?" Cf. Daniel, *Le temps qui reste,* Paris (Stock), 1973.

I
The Swiss Empire

1
How United
are the Barons?

Of the great men of this world
We declaim heroic songs –
How, rising up like stars,
They fall like stars.

Bertolt Brecht
Die Ballade vom Wasserrad

What is imperialism? In 1916, sitting in the vaulted gloom of
Zürich's Predigerkirche, by then a municipal library, Lenin tried to
solve the following problem. The capitalist system feeds upon the
uninterrupted accumulation of capital, on the acceleration and intensification of production, the exploitation of available natural
resources, and on a rapid build-up of expertise in management,
technology and science. One day, this system enters what Lenin calls
the "monopoly" stage. That day has come in Switzerland and France
and the other industrialized countries of Europe, in the United States
and Japan. The accumulation of capital concentrates colossal wealth
in the hands of a few people. Competition between rival capitalist
groups tends to disappear. Monopolies come into existence: these
are groups of capitalists who dominate one or more specific economic sectors, in which they can do what they please. Now monopolies
have a natural tendency to expand. They are based on the maximization of profit and on continuous growth. Monopolies are conquer-
ing the world, driving out pre-capitalist production methods everywhere. They snap up markets on all five continents, take over the
areas where raw materials are produced, and – with non-capitalist
production methods – they destroy whole civilizations. In short,
they are making a world in their own image.

Max Horkheimer says: "Henceforth, all history is the history
of things bought and sold." What is in fact being bought and sold is
finance capital. This consists of industrial and banking capital, and
in the hands of those who wield it, it becomes a weapon of terrifying
effectiveness. In each hegemonic capitalist country at the centre, the

17

small group of people that owns, uses, and controls the strategy of finance capital may be called the oligarchy.

There are two preliminary problems to consider. First, is there such a thing as secondary imperialism as a specific entity different from primary imperialism? Or is secondary imperialism merely a kind of ward of primary imperialism, totally dependent upon it, just the next step down in the world hierarchy of patronage and profit? The first sociologists of imperialism gave a single and unequivocal answer to this question: there is absolutely *no* specific difference. Secondary imperialism, they said, is common-or-garden imperialism, and is in no way distinct from any putative primary imperialism. However, since they made their analyses,[1] the social landscape of our planet has changed in several important respects. The problem now presents itself in different terms and must be looked at afresh.

The second problem is as follows. Imperialism is the ultimate stage of capitalist development. It *is* capitalism. In it we find the innermost rationale of capitalism, its most visible ambition, its most murderous possibilities. It will disappear only when the capitalist system itself does. Yet imperialism, with its policies, aggression, and institutionalized violence, also exists in our world alongside other forms of foreign policy, such as those pursued by the socialist states.

This book is about the secondary imperialism of Switzerland. Switzerland is part of the worldwide capitalist system. In this sense, the term "secondary imperialism" relates back to the primary imperialism of the North American oligarchy.[2]

I spoke, in my Introduction, of the crisis of imperialism – a crisis of adjustment and reconstruction, demanded by the rise of a new agent of aggression against the poor nations: the multinational capitalist enterprise. Such enterprises were born from the gradual development of finance capital into worldwide monopolies.

This new factor has produced profound changes in the social fabric of our world. I will try to indicate the most important of these.

The increasing penetration of multinational enterprises into a state on the periphery results in the destruction of that state's political system and institutions. From the earliest days of colonial conquest, the hegemonic metropolitan state planned and set up capitalist states in the colonized areas; and though the requirements governing the creation of the peripheral state were those of imperialist capitalism, they were mediated by a local superstructure. Today, the peripheral states are being subjected to a quite unforeseen attack, and in most cases are succumbing to it. It is the multinational com-

18

panies themselves that mount the attack, when they find obstacles to their penetration and profit-making being set up by a peripheral capitalist state which they consider inefficient.

The examples of Brazil and Chile, which recur several times in this book, form a sound basis for generalization. In fact, it would be a matter of indifference whether we took the case of South Korea, Bolivia, Zaïre, Guatemala or Indonesia, in order to demonstrate how the political society of the periphery is destroyed, and replaced by a fascist dictatorship composed of mercenaries equipped, financed and indoctrinated by the primary imperialist metropolis and the multinational companies of the secondary metropolises. Throughout the Third World the pattern is the same: the multinational companies replace the capitalist state at the centre as agents of imperialist aggression, and in the peripheral nations this leads to the disappearance of their former heterogeneous political societies. In the countries of the Persian Gulf and Central Arabia, there have never been heterogeneous systems. But in places like Chile before 1973 or Brazil before 1964, where open and complex political systems did exist, the resistance to imperialist penetration was broken by the multinational companies themselves. What has been set up is a despotic system of a totally new sort: a dictatorship by local officers trained in the establishments for practical training and indoctrination run by the imperialist centres (the American zone of Panama, American schools of counter-insurgency in the north of Thailand, etc.). This new system of despotism gives the tutelary multinational societies the most efficient and profitable opportunities for their super-exploitation of peoples who are kept repressed by their own soldiers.[3]

The redeployment of imperialism also produces other consequences. Chief among them are the destruction of the production and consumption cycle of the traditional capitalism of the periphery, as it emerged from the colonial period,[4] and the break-up of the traditional hierarchy of the dominated population as new patterns of capital movement are established between the local ruling class and the banking empires of the metropolis. This is a process we must look at more closely.

In the Third World, multinational enterprise directs its activities in relation to the "needs", or more precisely the consumption patterns, of the upper and upper-middle classes of the countries concerned. Naturally it is not concerned with the real and urgent needs of the undernourished masses whose incomes are too low to bring them into the market. It is the purchasing power of the well-off that determines the price structure, the investment strategy and the distribution system that are established; one has only to look at the way baby-food is distributed by the Nestlé Company in Chile, Colombia and Guatemala – all countries where infant malnutrition is appalling.[5] But the upper and upper-middle classes of the poor countries do not develop their own consumption patterns. Their behaviour is sheer imitation, mimicking the consumption patterns (the commodities, the status-symbols, etc.) of the ruling classes in their respective imperialist centres. The results of this mimicry by the ruling classes on the periphery are disastrous, for these patterns are then imposed on the middle and poor classes whose own material and cultural consumption patterns are thereby destroyed, causing them to become impoverished, de-cultured and destitute.[6]

Similarly, multinational enterprise imposes on the periphery all the most sophisticated techniques of industrialization, agriculture, trade and services. The rapid increase in production and the accumulation of short-term capital that result from technological rationalization are achieved at the expense of the workers. A dual society comes into being, marked by the uneasy coexistence in a single nation of two mutually opposed societies: a minority society of intensive consumption, dominating another society comprising the majority of the people, lacking in the most basic essentials – food, medical care, education, housing, social mobility. The strategy pursued by the multinationals can only accentuate the contradiction.

As we can see from the analyses of Strahm and Kappeler (following this chapter and the next), the intensification of industrial and agricultural production, advances in technology and massive capital investment do not, under these conditions, bring any economic and social progress to a country. For the accumulation of capital that results from expanding the production mechanism is in the hands of a tiny minority of the local population and of the multinational companies.

I shall be demonstrating later how the capital accumulated by the ruling classes in the Third World flows continually out to the "safe" reinvestment circuits offered by the banking monopolies at the centre. The consequence of the failure to establish a national capital invested at home is evident around all the major urban centres of Latin America, Asia and Africa. A destitute mass, an army of unemployed men, undernourished women and children, is huddled round the edges of the residential areas, beneath the skyscrapers, outside the parks and gardens of the propertied classes. These are the outcasts. What is radically new about this historical phenomenon is that this lumpen-proletariat, instead of getting gradually smaller as the capitalism of the periphery develops, is growing all the time. More and more of the dominated keep being sucked into the social vacuum, cast out along the roads, displaced into the shanty-towns. These creatures of the night are the direct victims of the combined action of the international companies and their political tools on the spot. They have reached new depths of degradation : [7] these millions of people – in Latin America they make up some 40 per cent of the population – have *no function at all*, either social or economic; they no longer even figure statistically as beasts of burden, for the logic of the new imperialist system decrees that they be identity-less, homeless, workless, in other words, that they be non-existent.

It is important to recognize the cultural imperialism that underlies, and thus also justifies, economic and political imperialism. If capital is the same the world over, then there must necessarily be a single set of values as laid down by the oligarchy at the centre. This single, worldwide, dominant ideology serves the purpose of creating the cultural, intellectual and psychological conditions for imperialism to operate unchecked. In a striking phrase, Piettre calls it the "imperialism of the vacuum".[8] For, indeed, the imperialism of multinational hegemonic capital, unlike the old state imperialism, is not the bearer of an alternative civilization. It destroys by fire and the sword – or, more literally, by the military take-over of universities, by indoctrinating the local ruling classes in management technology, by total control of the press and other local communications media – the culture (or cultures) of the conquered, the class ideology (or ideologies) that governed the old heterogeneous society. And what does it replace them with? *Nothing.* Or, to be more precise, with a commercial language that reduces man purely to his buying and selling functions, and leaves him no independent meaning, no personal future, none of the elementary cultural weapons to resist the new values imposed by capital.[9]

It is therefore a monopoly of knowledge – technological, experimental, scientific knowledge, and consequently ethnocentric cultural knowledge trans-substantiated into a Universal Knowledge – supported by money and weaponry, and generated by the multinational enterprises at the centre, that today almost totally ensures the economic, political, cultural and existential dependence of the subject peoples. To Marx, knowledge was one productive force among others. Since the second industrial revolution, the discovery of atomic fission and the exploration of outer space, the evidence seems to me to suggest that knowledge has become the first and foremost of all productive forces. This must be emphasised: not only is the scientific knowledge of subject peoples controlled today by capitalist transnational enterprises, but also their approach to problems (i.e. *which* problems will concern them), their emotions and their sensitivities.

All knowledge, of course, has a history: every science began somewhere. All knowledge was originally related to solving the problems of a society, a particular group of people. Furthermore, what I find most striking in the statements of directors of international firms is the way they identify themselves and their companies with a definite sense of nationality.[10] The international companies always refer to themselves as American, French, Japanese, Swiss, etc. The question is whether this is a ruse, a tactic for concealing their own strategy of world domination beneath a patriotic mask of pretended national identity. Or is it one of those phenomena of "mental lag" referred to by Marx, which prove that man's cognitive structures always lag behind his practical experience? A third possibility seems to me more plausible: the international firm, that major new agent of imperialist aggression, like every other sector of present-day capitalist society, starts from a cultural background that is to some extent autonomous and pre-dated the advent of hegemonic capital. For instance: American imperialism was shaped as much by the aggressive Calvinism of the Pilgrim Fathers as by the logic inherent in American capitalist accumulation (and all its by-products, like Taylorism, behaviourism, sociological neo-positivism, etc.); the universalist humanism of the eighteenth-century French encyclopaedists[11] is vital to an understanding of the rise of French secondary imperialism. For every international firm, for every oppressive technology, one can point to an original cultural background. (But note: what I am interested in here is the knowledge controlled by the multinational companies, and therefore the social origins of that knowledge. I am not concerned with the individual backgrounds of particular directors of transnational empires. For instance, the present chairman of the Nestlé empire – the world's largest food company – is French, as is the president of IBM. What is important to understand is not the kind of education they had, the social indoctrination they have been through, but the social background and origin of the oppressive knowledge wielded by the companies they run. Nestlé in fact is "Swiss"; IBM is "American".)

Let us then return to the question we began with: has secondary imperialism a special social and symbolic nature and function of its own, or are all imperialisms identical in theory and in practice? I have mentioned one piece of empirical evidence – the subjective identification of the directors of international firms with the nations in which their firms originated. But this is hardly enough. We must move beyond this sort of "collective subjectivity" and get down to analysing the power relations that objectively determine what the primary and secondary oligarchies actually do.

To take one example: if the USA suddenly renounced its domination of Brazil – if, in other words, it stopped financing, equipping and indoctrinating the army, the police and the whole manifold apparatus for repressing trade unions and popular organizations – could Swiss firms in Brazil continue making the fantastic profits they have been drawing ever since the Brazilian Institutional Act was enacted in 1968?[12] Of course not. Military dictatorship, unconcealed terror and torture are indispensable conditions for the foreign multinational companies to exploit the country's resources and human labour as outrageously as they do. If there were no terror, then the people would rise to demand a decent minimum wage, an equitable taxation system, investment in the social infrastructure. However, there is terror; and therefore there is no possibility of wage negotiation and no job security in Brazil today. In the seven states of the north-east, 52 per cent of the children die of malnutrition before the age of five.[13] Hundreds of thousands more go blind for lack of protein, yet some 30 per cent of the Brazilian national product is exported, and colossal fortunes are made year after year by the multinational oligarchy.

To take this a step further: a military dictatorship like the one the USA has set up in Brazil cannot function in isolation. Similar régimes must be established around its borders, so as to prevent tensions or threats of instability from arising elsewhere on the continent. In Uruguay, Bolivia and Chile, an iron cordon of satellite dictatorships now surrounds the unhappy peoples of the southern part of the Latin American continent. Obviously none of the secondary European or Japanese imperialisms operating in the area possesses the financial or military means to create such a set-up. Since our study concerns Switzerland, we can say that the Swiss state has neither a powerful enough army nor adequate financial means, nor, finally, the position on the international chessboard that would enable it to establish its own zones of domination in Latin America, in Asia, in Australasia or in Africa. Switzerland does not even have an ideology of aggression. The neutralist ideology by which

23

it lives is non-imperialist, supports the principle of nationality, and is in some ways, paradoxically, cosmopolitan. The federalist and decentralized structure of the state, and an ideology in which mercantile protestantism is combined with scrupulous respect for the varied ethnic origins of the inhabitants, certainly do not provide the Swiss oligarchy with the intellectual equipment for explaining or legitimating their daily aggression against the poor nations.

Therefore, any analysis of the interaction of North American primary imperialism and Swiss secondary imperialism in Brazil suggests – at least at first sight – that the secondary is totally dependent on the primary. But in fact the relationship is somewhat more complex: there are serious contradictions between the activities of the two oligarchies. They are evident both at the centre – in Switzerland – and at the periphery. I will indicate a few of them.

The oligarchy, which is the social face and dominant ideological forum of hegemonic capitalism, comes into being in the final phase of over-accumulation, of maximization of profit and intensified exploitation of surplus-value. It comprises those capitalists who, because of (a) the great proportion of the vital means of production that they own and (b) their personal wealth, exercise unquestioned dominance over the options and aims of the accumulation process. In Switzerland the oligarchs are, with very few exceptions, members of patrician families whose immense fortunes come from primitive accumulation.

Let us look more closely at these two "qualifications" for membership. First: the oligarchy owns the greater part of the means of production. Between those who manage the Swiss multinational empires and those who own them, the separation is clear and complete.

For example: the most powerful pharmaceutical trust in the world, Hoffmann-La Roche SA of Basle, belongs to three families, the Hoffmanns, the Oeris and the Sachers. These three families collect over sixteen million Swiss francs a year, solely in the shape of dividends. The general manager of Hoffmann-La Roche is a man called Adolf W. Jann. None of his sons has a directorship, but the heads of the three families all have seats on the board. This system means that none of their managers, however ambitious, can ever contest their omnipotence. Astronomic though his salary may be, the manager is never more than an employee of the ruling families.

There is one exception that proves the rule: Philippe de Weck, the general manager of the Union Bank of Switzerland (Union de banque suisse), declares an annual net income of 1.2 million

Swiss francs. He is one of the most powerful managers in the world. At the same time, he has a share in the ownership of the means of production he manages, for he is in fact one of the largest shareholders in the same bank. There are two reasons for this: he managed to sell his family bank, the Banque de Weck in Fribourg, to the Union Bank of Switzerland, and get himself paid in shares. Furthermore, he had the good sense to marry the daughter of the Genevan banker de Saussure, thus acquiring another considerable block of shares. I must repeat: de Weck is the exception; Jann is the rule. There is no real movement between the closed world of even the topmost management and that of the ultra-suspicious oligarchs.

However, another kind of upheaval can occur. One powerful family in the oligarchy may find itself done down by another. For example: the Bally family of Schoenenwerd owns and manages one of the most powerful industrial holdings of Europe (shoes, chemicals, etc.). They were involved with other Zürich families in establishing the Union Bank of Switzerland. But following a too-rapid expansion, the Schoenenwerd trust is now dominated by the Union Bank of Switzerland – actually a coalition of oligarchs hostile to the Ballys.

The second qualification for membership is quite straight-forward: overwhelming personal wealth. For example, the amount of wealth inside Switzerland is reckoned to be 226 billion Swiss francs, and 3.3 per cent of the population alone control over half of it.[14]

> Ah, we had so many masters,
> We had tigers and hyenas,
> We had pigs and we had eagles.[15]

But Brecht is wrong: there are few "masters" in Switzerland today. Though they may be "eagles" and "tigers", they tend to appear in the harmless guise of well-bred bourgeois – cultivated, a bit humdrum, humane, intelligent, astute, pious. There are still a few obvious tigers, though: Max Schmidheiny, king of cement and banking (Holderbank Trust and Crédit Suisse), Dieter Bührle (the arms merchant), Dieter Wolfer (of the multinational Diesel engine company, Locomotives Sulzer SA), Hans R. Schwarzenbach and Alfred R. Sulzer who control worldwide empires of textiles, foodstuffs and machine tools (Robert Schwarzenbach Holding SA, Nestlé, Sulzer SA). These last three control the Union Bank of Switzerland. There is one among all the oligarchs past and present for whom I have a soft spot, indeed even, oddly enough, a real sympathy: Corthésy, once the ruler of the Nestlé-Alimentana empire. In 1968 I happened by pure chance to be with him on a flight across the South Atlantic. Corthésy and his entourage were making a state visit to their colonies in Brazil. He presented such a splendid combination of imperial arrogance and Calvinist modesty. Enthroned in his first-class seat in the front of the Boeing, with his enormous feet encased in unmistakably Swiss slippers and his shirt-sleeves rolled up, the sovereign loudly summoned one after another of his satraps from their seats in the economy class to confer with him.

Should one attempt a psychological analysis of the aristocracy of hegemonic capitalism? Do we need that in order to understand the strategies and tactics of Swiss secondary imperialism? Not really. This secondary imperialism, like all imperialism, arises out of a structural violence. History is actually made by finance capital. All the people – *all* of them – are interchangeable. The men who constitute the oligarchy are reducible to the way they fulfil their function, or more accurately, to the way they conform to the commercial hegemonic model. I must stress this point: we are not concerned here with psychological variations, with how much of the actual faces one can see. Some early works on secondary imperialism set out to identify all the actors individually. For example: Fritz Giovanoli compiled a list of some two hundred people who held most of the key positions in the economy.[16] Since his book was published, the concentration of capital has become narrower. If we make a comparative study of the members of boards, we find a kind of power élite of *twenty-six individuals* whose influence extends to every key sector of the oligarchy's domination of the economy.[17] These people control vast amounts of money, and wield a power that is as unseen as it is violent and effective.

For example:[18] in 1974, the balance-sheets of only the five largest multinational commercial banks, whose headquarters are in Zürich, Basle or Berne, amounted to over 125 billion Swiss francs. The Swiss GNP for that year was around 144 billion. There are over four thousand banks in Switzerland: thus only *five* of them control a volume of money not far short of the sum-total of all the wealth produced in Switzerland in a year.[19] These banking empires control sums ten times the size of the national budget (the federal budget for 1974 was 12 billion francs). The Union Bank of Switzerland in 1974 made a profit of around 183 million; the Swiss Bank Corporation, 178 million; and the Crédit Suisse (Swiss Credit Bank) 156 million.

It is not just the amount of money involved, but the extent of the worldwide network of exploitation created by the barons of cement, chemicals and banking, that indicates the extent of the sheer strength exercised by the Swiss oligarchy: Switzerland is the home of 447 multinational companies controlling 1,456 subsidiaries; 85.7 per cent of those subsidiaries are in the industrial countries of the centre, 14.3 per cent in the Third World.[20]

The following table lists the chief "Swiss" multinational companies, with the percentage of each one's turnover attributable to foreign trade:[21]

Nestlé	98%	BBC	76%
Continental Linoleum	91%	Schindler	67%
Ciba-Geigy	85%	Sika Konzern	66%
Unikeller Holding	85%	Holzstoff	65%
Holderbank	84%	Luwa	61%
Hoffmann-La Roche	80%	Georg Fischer	48%
Sandoz	80%	Sulzer	46%
Interfood	80%	Oerlikon-Bührle	43%
Alusuisse	80%		

However, to return to our original question, impressive though the economic and financial power of the secondary oligarchy appears, and widespread as is their network of exploitation, their power is nothing in comparison with that of the North American oligarchy. The latter impose their law upon the Swiss imperialist oligarchy, and they are established in Switzerland on a massive scale and against the wishes of the local oligarchy. They are almost always victorious when they compete with Swiss banks and trusts for the domination of the home market, as well as in winning the most fertile areas of the periphery (such as South Africa and Brazil). In November 1974, they forced Switzerland virtually to abandon its independent petroleum policy and to join the International Energy Agency – a fighting cartel under American leadership which is directed against the oil-producing countries.

The primary oligarchy needs to be supplied with capital from the Swiss market. For example: Honeywell, a multinational manufacturer of what are known as "anti-personnel" weapons (fragmentation bombs, etc.), and Dow Chemical, a multinational manufacturer of napalm, contract their loans in Switzerland. The American government has succeeeded in getting Swiss banking law ch in 1974, it forced the Federal Council to sign a so-ca mutual assistance" agreement, whereby Swiss banks upon to open their records to American investigators.

The network of merchant banks which is the basis of all Swiss economic life is also marked by competition between the primary and secondary oligarchies. Here are a few figures: at the end of 1973, there were 99 foreign banks in Switzerland, dominated in the main by American capital; 84 of them were foreign-owned (though registered in Switzerland) and the remaining 15 were branches of

Switzerland, a country very much geared to foreign trade, has intensive trade relationships with the developing countries: in 1971 there were 4.9 billion Swiss francs' worth of exports, and only 2.6 million of imports (cf. "Direction fédérale des douanes, statistique suisse du commerce extérieur, rapport annuel", 1971, Part I, Berne, 1972). Switzerland is thus distinguished, in its relationship with the Third World, by a (structural) surplus of 2.3 billion Swiss francs. The developing countries offer enormous openings to Swiss export industry. Over the last decade, over 20 per cent of Swiss exports have regularly gone to these countries (cf. "Message du conseil fédéral à l'assemblée fédérale sur la politique du marché de la Suisse face aux pays en voie de développement, en particulier sur la participation en faveur de ces pays", 24 March 1971, p. 10). Thus the contribution of the Third World to the prosperity of Switzerland far exceeds the aid, whether public or private, bestowed by Switzerland on the Third World on supposedly preferential terms.

The favourable sum-total of this balance-sheet is not due solely to the output capacity of the Swiss export industry, even combined with all the official encouragement it receives. Carefully placed obstacles have managed to cut down the import of products from the developing countries. It is worth making a brief excursus here to examine some of the important features of Swiss customs regulations.

1. Protective tariffs. This tariff, calculated according to the surplus value of a particular process of production, is twice the nominal customs rate usually cited as evidence of the low rates of duty levied by Swiss customs. Until certain tariff preferences were granted, it represented a considerable handicap to trade for Third World products. The fact that customs rates rise in proportion to the degree of complexity of the commodity imported reduces the chances of a developing country's becoming successfully industrialized.

2. The tax reductions granted for products imported from the developing countries during the "Kennedy round" of Gatt offered on average no greater preference than those granted to the same products by the other industrialized countries.

3. Unlike most industrialized countries, Switzerland bases its import duties not on the value, but on the *weight* of the goods being imported; there are therefore heavier taxes on cheaper goods. The disadvantage of this for the developing countries is obvious. Lower wages and poorer quality often combine to produce a lower retail price than that of rival products in the industrialized countries. That is why customs duties on the main products from the Third World – such as wool, cotton or leather – represent a burden $1\frac{1}{2}$ to $2\frac{1}{2}$ times heavier than on the corresponding products from industrialized countries. (Hollenstein, *op. cit.*).

foreign firms (with no independent legal existence).[22] With the relative collapse of the dollar, and the establishment of the overvalued Swiss franc as international reserve currency, the number of banks under foreign control, as well as of local branches of foreign banks, is likely to increase. Banks, finance companies, investment trusts, currency speculators and discreet firms offering dubious brokering services – some Swiss, some foreign – are locked in a battle in which virtually no holds are barred.[23]

Or, to take another example: the Swiss banking empires are the chief moneylenders to the racist régime in South Africa. Since the draconian laws in force there guarantee the exploitation of the black workers, there is no shortage of industrial establishments belonging (via holding companies) to finance groups in Geneva, Zürich and Basle. To illustrate the sort of exploitation that goes on, let us simply note the *Guardian* (29 March 1973) report of how on the previous day, 700 black workers at the South African branch of a Swiss-based multinational went on strike against their inhuman working conditions. The management of Alusuisse[24] (for this was the company in question) refused to negotiate with the strikers and sacked all of them. In addition, it appealed to the government against its own workers: a contingent of a hundred armed police was sent, which put down the workers with bloodshed.

A fierce struggle is taking place today in South Africa between the North American multinationals and the secondary imperialism of the Swiss, to gain control of finance capital. The result is that the USA publicly denounces the apartheid régime. The Swiss multinationals have found a novel solution: they are transferring those stages of production in which the workers are most outrageously exploited out of South Africa altogether – to Port Louis, in Mauritius. There the multinational companies have established a "duty-free zone", where thousands of tons of semi-finished products are unloaded every year. Here they are finished by a labour-force of women who work for even more scandalous wages, and in even more appalling conditions of hygiene and safety. The finished products are then re-exported to western Europe, mainly to the Common Market countries, via Great Britain.[25]

There are, then, very real conflicts of interest. But in the final analysis they are only secondary. What governs all the dealings between the primary and secondary oligarchies is their functional unity. Swiss (or French, or Japanese, or whatever) secondary imperialism fulfils specific and indispensable functions within what is a single system of world domination; we are looking in particular at the Swiss case. That functional unity takes precedence over all the competitive elements in the parallel activities of the various

Swiss foreign credits rose to 166 billion francs in 1970. We must subtract from this 86 billion francs of foreign capital in Switzerland – which leaves 80 billion net in Swiss credits abroad. If this were equally divided up, it would give every inhabitant of the country 14,400 francs – which far exceeds the American average of 1,500 francs a head for capital invested abroad. (According to H. Kleinewefers, in the *Neue Zürcher Zeitung*, 13 January 1972, Swiss credits abroad are considerably less than the figures I give here, which are those given by Max Ikle.) This wealth outside the country is distributed among industrial firms (manufacture), stocks and shares, insurance, real estate and bank credits – the latter representing the larger part of the total. In that same year, banks operating in Switzerland received 53 billion francs from abroad, and themselves sent 66 billion francs abroad. The key position of the three major Swiss banks is clearly indicated here, since a large proportion of this money passes through their accounts (Swiss Bank Corporation, Union Bank of Switzerland and Crédit Suisse).

As a creditor, then, Switzerland is in a strong position which naturally affects its income abroad. The rough estimate is instructive on this point. The earnings from capital (interest, dividends), after deduction of Swiss interest paid abroad, rose in 1971 to 3,500 million francs. The Swiss banks received over 500 million in commission and taxes and 100 million from their own money invested abroad in stocks and shares. Including the 340 million francs coming in from insurance abroad, Swiss capital abroad brought in around $4\frac{1}{2}$ billion francs in 1971; to this must be added probably over a billion from royalties and licensing rights. The total sum must therefore finally have been over $5\frac{1}{2}$ billion – or 6 per cent of the national income. However, these figures tell us nothing about Swiss holdings in the Third World at least as regards banking and insurance. To lift a corner of the veil, one must study the international markets in which the three largest Swiss banks hold a major position. (Beat Kappeler, *op. cit.*)

imperialisms of our day. Or to put it in another way, it fixes the tolerable limits of any real confrontation, competition or conflict between the two oligarchies. Such conflicts are never allowed to pose any real threat to the world system of domination, at least not as long as they can be handled – which seems, as far as one can see, to be the case at present – within the framework of the strategic unity of the imperialist states. When they become a danger to the secondary oligarchy, the latter deal with the problem by shaping their strategy within a supranational organization of some kind, such as the European Common Market or the International Energy Agency.

It is important to stress this point, which accounts for the ambiguous nature of secondary imperialism: continually at risk of being turned into a satellite, its relative and paradoxical independence is growing ever more precarious; yet the more its independence is undermined, the more dedicated does the secondary oligarchy become to its role of indispensable assistant and instrument of primary imperialism. The paradox is only apparent: imperialism, by its very nature, imposes absolute choices which, once made, are almost irrevocable. Though it is true that the two oligarchies – the American and the Swiss – may well be competitors in one market, it is perfectly clear that both, whether their situation be one of conflict or of complementarity, have their origins in the same contradictory political and economic system in which our world is organized. The banking, industrial, military, commercial and political strategy of all the imperialist oligarchies, whether primary or secondary, is always and everywhere the same: it is one of monopolistic domination of markets, of maximization of profits, and of massive exploitation of human beings.

Notes to Chapter 1

1. In particular Lenin's *Imperialism, the Highest Stage of Capitalism,* written in the spring of 1916 in Zürich; Rosa Luxemburg's *The Accumulation of Capital,* published in 1931; Bukharin's *World Economy and Imperialism* (expanded from an article he wrote for the review *The Communist* in 1915).

2. I leave aside here the debate on whether or not Soviet power has an imperialist character; for a lucid study of this problem cf. "Mao Tsé-Toung et l'Union soviétique" (texts and commentaries) in an appendix to Alain Bouc's *Mao Tsé-Toung ou la Révolution approfondie,* Paris (Seuil), 1975, pp.226ff. See also J.-F.Revel, *La Tentation totalitaire,* Paris (Laffont), 1976; and E.Morin, *Autocritique,* Paris (Seuil), 1970.

3. For a well worked-out theory of change in the peripheral states, cf. A.Touraine, *Production de la société,* Paris (Seuil), 1973.

4. For an understanding of the way the economies of the periphery are gradually destroyed by the multinational companies, I am indebted to Dan Galin, the general secretary of the UITA (Union internationale des travailleurs de l'alimentation), Charles Levinson, of the International Chemical Workers' Union, and Dan Benedict, of the International Steelworkers' Union. Their three organizations all have their headquarters in Geneva.

5. This multinational food company has a strategy of monopolizing the production of milk and citrus fruits in whatever countries it becomes established. Then, in each country, it manufactures a range of food for infants (milk, powdered soups, baby-foods) whose price is geared to the purchasing power of the upper middle and upper classes. The (unintended) consequence of this is that the comfortably-off are supplied with new and high-quality products, while the poor, because they are excluded from the market, see the malnutrition among their children growing worse. Cf. the analysis, "Nestlé", published periodically by the UITA in Geneva.

6. For a good theory of de-culturization, cf. G.Balandier, *Sens et Puissance,* Paris (PUF), 1972; J.Duvignaud, *Le Langage perdu,* Paris (PUF), 1973.

7. No family or social structure can withstand this degradation. In Sri-Lanka the proletariat of the multinational tea plantations are forced to sell their children to give them a chance of physical survival. Cf. the *Sunday Times* enquiry of 30 March 1975.

8. A.Piettre, "Impérialisme et culture", *Le Monde,* 3 May 1975, p.4.

9. To quote from Anouar Abdel-Malek: "It really seems that what is involved today is something far more important: the control of the process whereby world development is directed, regulated and decided, by the advanced nations' monopoly of scientific knowledge and ideological creativity." Further on he says that imperialism is today in a position "to affect the innermost personality of peoples, nations and cultures, and above all to determine the area of problems they will be concerned with and the emotional colouring of their feelings." And again: "The combined action of the military-industrial complex and of the cultural centres of Western domination, as a result of the advanced stage of development of monopoly finance capital, and most important, of the industrial revolution, is what determines the content of imperialism in our time: it is, in sober truth, a hegemonic imperialism, the highest stage of well-organised violence in the history of mankind. It depends on fire and the sword, of course, but it also seeks to control people's ideas and feelings." Cf. A.Abdel-Malek, "Pour une sociologie de l'impérialisme", in *L'Homme et la Société,* no. 6, pp.290-91.

10. Isaiah Berlin, "The Bent Twig, a Note on Nationalism", in *Foreign Affairs,* vol. 51, 1 October 1972, pp.11ff.

11. This is merely to touch on a vast debate. I have not the space here to

defend my position. Some will say that my argument is fallacious, and that the Calvinism of the sixteenth century in Europe and the universalism of the eighteenth-century encyclopaedists were both simply ideological patterns produced and determined by two successive phases in European capitalist accumulation. I can only refer them to Roger Bastide's theory of autonomous collective subjectivities, which I myself find totally convincing.

12. M.Arruda *et al., Multinationals and Brazil,* with a preface by R.Barnet, published by Brazilian Studies, Toronto, 1975.

13. "Mortalidade infantil no Nordeste", *Jornal do Brasil,* 16 August 1974.

14. Figures from C.M.Holliger, *Die Reichen und die Superreichen in der Schweiz* (Hoffmann & Campe), 1974.

15. Brecht, *Die Ballade vom Wasserad.*

16. Cf. G. Giovanoli, *Libre Suisse, voici tes maîtres* (Socialist Party publication), Zürich, 1939.

17. For a detailed analysis of boards of directors, cf. *Revue Focus,* Zürich, 1974.

18. All figures relating to the Gross National Product come from the Federal Assembly's documentation service. However, they are never more than approximate, and there are divergences, some of them significant. There are two reasons for this: in any case the system of statistics in Switzerland is very poor (because of the deliberate, structural impenetrability of the economy), and further to that, there is a serious problem of falsification of balance-sheets. Cf. P.Del Boca, *Le Faux Bilan de la société anonyme* (doctoral thesis), Lausanne.

19. *Les Banques suisses en 1974,* Study no. 59, from the statistical and information service of the Banque nationale suisse, p.96ff.

20. These figures are from the UN document referred to in note 7 of the Introduction. For the volume, location and structure of Swiss private industrial investment in the developing countries, see the appendix to this chapter.

21. This table is given by P.Nobel, "Solidarität oder Rentabilität?", *Schweiz-Dritte Welt,* a symposium, Zürich (Schulthess), 1973, p.133.

22. Figures from the *Bulletin de l'Association des banques étrangères en Suisse* published yearly in June.

23. Swiss legislation for the status and operation of foreign banks is notoriously inadequate. There is a simple reason: most foreign firms in Switzerland are set up as *sociétés anonymes,* and the *Code des obligations* demands that such companies have a majority of Swiss directors on the board. Thus, numbers of foreign banks, finance companies, etc., recruit parliamentarians, party leaders, company lawyers and local bigwigs – just as their Swiss counterparts do. Such men are naturally tempted to see that no serious restrictions are placed on foreign (or Swiss) banking activities.

24. Alusuisse is a multinational company dealing in bauxite, alumina and aluminium: it made a profit of 204 million Swiss francs in 1974.

25. For details of the operation, cf. *Afrique-Asie,* 1973.

Appendix to Chapter 1

(To understand the "autonomous" power of Swiss industrial capital, one must be able to define its axes of penetration in the Third World. Text and tables are from Rudolf Strahm.[1] J.Z.)

Extent and location of industrial investments

At the end of 1972, the assessable value of Swiss private investment in the Third World was around four billion Swiss francs.[2] The most recent study of the distribution of direct investment was made by the OECD in 1967.[3]

Table 1 shows the geographical distribution of the direct private investments from Switzerland and the sixteen western industrial member-countries of the DAC (Development Assistance Committee, an OECD body). Switzerland, with almost 2 per cent of the overall investment in the developing countries, is represented in southern Europe (which comes within the OECD definition of a developing area) and Latin America with respective averages of over 6.5 per cent and over 2.3 per cent. It is somewhat lower than this (0.9 per cent to 1 per cent) in Africa and Asia, where the poverty is far greater. However, in South Africa (which does not figure in the total), Hong Kong, Thailand, Formosa, Singapore and South Korea, as well as Argentina, Mexico, Brazil and the West Indies, the Swiss involvement is above average. Of all the Afro-Asian countries, only one of those states classified as among the poorest has a higher than average Swiss investment, and that is Guinea, where the subsoil is of interest because of the bauxite. Switzerland has established considerable industries there based on bauxite extraction (Alusuisse).

Swiss investments are effectively channelled into a small number of countries. A study made by the trade division of the Federal Department of the Economy (whose findings do not coincide exactly with those of the OECD study) in 1968 revealed that 58 per cent of all Swiss investment in the Third World (and southern Europe) is concentrated in four countries: Brazil (19.2 per cent), Spain (15.1 per cent), Argentina (12.24 per cent) and Mexico (11.5 per cent). Which means that 43 per cent go to benefit the three most prosperous states in Latin America.

With good capitalist logic, Swiss capital invests in those countries and areas of the Third World which are relatively advanced industrially, and offer the possibility of a "free" economy in a politically "stable" climate. The only exceptions to this are mining industries which are of necessity tied to natural conditions (like Alusuisse, in Guinea). The sectors of the economy favoured by the Swiss follow a classification by which first place (still in assessable value) is accorded to processing industries – which represent 55 per cent of all Swiss investment. Next come the various sectors of the infrastructure (especially electricity) with 16 per cent; then trading with 7 per cent; the remainder goes in tourism, banking and mines.

The presence of Swiss capital in the developing countries is evident from the large number of Swiss firms established in them. The five largest international trusts in Switzerland control, at the lowest estimate, 161 subsidiaries and plants in the developing countries, and the nine largest control 192.

Table II shows the majority involvements (50 per cent and above of the capital) of ten Swiss trusts in developing countries (excluding southern Europe). This does not include subsidiaries that are only sales outlets or centres of distribution; nor does it include the forty or so factories under Swiss control in South Africa. We have only imprecise information about Hoffmann-La Roche and its investments. Nor can we claim to have compiled a complete list, given that it is seldom easy to establish the distinction either between majority shareholding and effective control via minority shareholding, or between production industries and distribution centres.[4]

The involvement of Swiss finance companies and holding companies operating from Switzerland is not included.[5] Of the thousand American holding companies which control US firms and their subsidiaries throughout the world, *six hundred have their registered offices in Switzerland*, for reasons, obviously enough, of taxation convenience.[6]

The largest of all is the Nestlé Company which is among the world giants, with 297 factories throughout the world, 81 of which are in 28 developing countries. With 100 administrative centres and 697 marketing centres all over the world, Nestlé could well be the most multinational of all the worldwide trusts, in terms of sheer geographical dispersal. Nestlé's domination operates from three different domains: Nestlé Alimentana SA includes the parent establishment at Vevey and controls the activities of the trust throughout Europe (apart from the sterling area); Nestlé Ltd covers the sterling area; Unilac Inc. controls activities in Panama and in all transatlantic countries (except the USA).

The total workforce employed by Swiss firms established in developing countries in 1971 amounted, according to figures supplied by the federal administration, to 100,700: 16,200 in the developing countries of southern Europe, 7,900 in Africa, 55,000 in Latin America and 21,600 in Asia.[7] About the distribution *by country* of the numbers employed by Swiss firms we know as little as we know about the sums they have invested in each country over the past few years. The most recent figures available for total Swiss investment in individual countries date from 1967. We base them on the OECD study mentioned above (cf. Table I). That study shows that figures could only be obtained in Switzerland by confidential enquiries, and that since 1968 they have been kept secret.

Table I The geographical distribution of private investment from Switzerland and all the DAC countries in the developing countries at the end of 1967. Figures in millions of dollars.

	Switzerland	Total from all DAC countries	Switzerland % of DAC total
Southern Europe	**130**	**1,993**	**6.5**
of which: Spain	110	1,377	8.0
Africa	**60**	**6,591**	**0.9**
of which: Guinea	19	93	20.5
Tanzania	3	60	5.0
excluding: South Africa (1966)	231	5,313	4.3
Central and South America	**427**	**18,449**	**2.3**
of which: Argentina	116	1,821	6.4
Dutch West Indies	21	381	5.5
Mexico	80	1,786	4.5
Brazil	140	3,728	3.8
Asia and the Middle East	**77**	**8,094**	**1.0**
of which: Thailand	8	214	3.7
Hong Kong	10	285	3.5
Taiwan	5	149	3.3
Singapore	5	183	2.7
South Korea	2	78	2.6
Total in the developing countries	**694**	**35,127**	**1.98**

Table II: Direct investments of the Swiss multinational companies in the developing countries (excepting southern Europe). Figures in millions of Swiss francs.

Company	Turnover	Workforce		Majority shareholdings in developing countries
		Total	In Switzerland	
Nestlé	15,770 (1972)	116,000	c. 6,000	**81 firms in 28 developing countries:** 66 in 14 countries in Latin America 10 in 6 countries in Asia 7 in 7 countries in Africa
Ciba-Geigy	8,064 (1972)	71,000	18,000	**29 firms in 21 developing countries:** 14 in 9 countries in Latin America 5 in 5 countries in Africa 10 in 7 countries in Asia and the Middle East
Hoffman-La Roche	5,500 (1971) approx. estimate	30,000	5,000	**16 firms in 12 developing countries:** 12 in 8 countries in Latin America 4 in 4 countries in Asia
BBC-Brown-Boveri	6,577 (1972)	92,000	19,000	**6 firms in 5 developing countries:** 2 in Brazil; 1 each in Argentia, Peru, Mexico and India
Sandoz	3,395 (1972)	32,000	9,000	**29 firms in 21 developing countries:** 16 in 11 countries in Latin America 10 in 7 countries in Asia and the Middle East 3 in 3 countries in Africa
Sulzer	2,150 (1970)	35,000	14,000	**12 firms in developing countries:** 6 in Latin America, 2 in Africa, 4 in Asia and the Middle East
Alusuisse	2,050 (1971)	25,000	4,000	**9 firms in 7 developing countries:** 2 in Brazil; 2 in Nigeria; 1 each in the Dutch West Indies, Costa Rica, Madagascar, Guinea and Sierra Leone
Holderbank	1,200 (1970)	9,600	1,400	**7 firms in 6 developing countries:** 2 in Costa Rica; 1 each in Mexico, Colombia, Brazil, Peru and Zaïre
Oerlikon-Bührle	1,109 (1972)	16,000		**3 firms in 3 developing countries:** 1 each in Brazil, Chile and Argentina; minority holdings in India, Pakistan, Sudan and Turkey

Notes to Appendix to Chapter 1

1. From the chapter on "Schweizer Industrieinvestitionen in Entwicklungsländern" in *Schweizer Kapital und dritte Welt.*

2. If we take the figure of 3,454 million at the end of 1968, published in *Investissements privés suisses dans le Tiers Monde* (a symposium, IUHEI, Geneva, 1971, p. 46), and add to it the investments annually recorded by the Department of Trade, we find a capital of 3,840 million Swiss francs at the end of 1971. To this must also be added the profits reinvested, reinvestments financed by loans, etc. The financial value of Swiss industrial investment in what are described as developing countries is thus much higher than the 4 billion or so declared officially.

3. OECD/Development Assistance Directorate, *Stock of Private Direct Investment by DAC Countries in Developing Countries,* OECD, Paris, 1972, pp.13-134.

4. Sources: the Management Reports of Nestlé, Ciba-Geigy, BBC, Sandoz, Alusuisse, Sulzer, Holderbank, Oerlikon-Bührle; also Hermann Stehler, *Politique d'investissement à l'étranger des grandes entreprises industrielles suisses,* St Gall, 1969; Max Ikle, *Le Suisse, rendez-vous des banques et de la finance internationale,* Zürich, 1970, p.171; Peter Nobel, "Entreprises multinationales", Büchi/Matter, *Suisse-Tiers Monde, solidarité ou rentabilité?* p.174; *Revue Focus,* no. 22, September 1971, Zürich, p.17.

5. Cf. Kappeler, *op. cit.*

6. OECD *op. cit.,* p.139.

7. *Entwicklung/Développement,* no. 17, January 1973.

2
"A Nation of Fences"

You know, my love, that Switzerland is called the silent strong-box,
full of fortunes that have been abstracted from somewhere or
something else. . . . Why have I written all this to you about
Switzerland? Perhaps out of envy for that little garden amid the
desert of blood. After all, have not the flowers in that little garden
been – are they not still? – watered by our blood flowing in the desert?
And in the peaceful snowy nights of Switzerland
Do not the stars glitter –
Watered by our tears?

Nazim Hikmet
En passant par la Suisse

A. Bankers and bandits: a network of channels

In the world imperialist system, Swiss imperialism plays the
vital role of the *fence*. The imperialist oligarchy in all the countries
at the centre, and their local accomplices in the countries on the
periphery (the ruling classes of peripheral capitalism), need somewhere where banking law, ease of converting currency, relative political stability, and technologically-advanced institutions that function
efficiently (telex, airports, accountancy systems) make it possible
first to safeguard, and then to reinvest profitably, their accumulated
plunder. There are two types of channel: the first is a system run
by the merchant banks themselves. These are usually extremely
well organized, and it is almost unheard-of for a banker to be caught.
(One exception, however, is the Geneva banker Hentsch, of Hentsch
and Co., a bank whose head office was in rue de la Corraterie. He
ran a network operating in Sweden, and was arrested by the Swedish
police in 1972, tried by the Göteborg Court and found guilty.) The
second is organized by professional "carriers", who arrange travel-
ling dates, commission terms, etc. They are paid by the clients who
export the capital, and deposit this illicit capital in Swiss banks. The
commission for Spanish pesetas, for instance, is currently 7 per cent
(cf. *Der Spiegel*, 19 January 1976), and the money is carried in suit-
cases, in 1,000-peseta notes.

No official figure has ever been given for the total amount of
dirty money from other countries stashed away in Switzerland. (By
"dirty money" I mean capital whose transfer does not relate to any
repayment of debt or trading transaction.) Even the Federal Council
say they do not know how much there is, where it comes from, or
where most of the astronomical sums are deposited. This poses an

interesting political problem: either the Swiss banks do not use accounting books, or the government does not know or want to know what goes on in its own country.

In 1974, the five major Swiss banking empires (Union Bank of Switzerland, Swiss Bank Corporation, Crédit Suisse, Banque Populaire and Banque Leu) alone controlled a turnover almost the same size as the gross national product. Now there are over four thousand banks in Switzerland (including all branches). The capital secreted in them has been withdrawn from liability to taxation in its countries of origin;[2] some of it is actually capital acquired by punishable criminal acts, some merely capital put in Switzerland for safe-keeping because its "security" seems more assured there than elsewhere. In most countries the export of capital in this way is forbidden. There are in Geneva a number of specialist "finance companies" that everyone knows about; both the networks controlled directly by banks or finance companies and those run by independent "transporters" make use of professional criminals and smugglers to do their work for them. Thus these networks are breaking numbers of laws, both Swiss and foreign, all the time. But the Swiss government strangely enough does nothing to dismantle them.

For example: the fall of the fascist dictatorship in Portugal on 24 April 1974 led to a massive flight of private capital. As soon as the first provisional government was formed, strict regulations were made to ban all non-authorized transfers of funds abroad. Yet, according to a report put out by the Bank of Portugal in July 1975, the country lost over a billion escudos in exported capital between April 1974 and April 1975. This was solely capital taken illegally out of the country (in cars with foreign number-plates, etc.) in banknotes. Those notes were later presented by the national banks of the (illegally) receiving countries to the Bank of Portugal to be converted into foreign currency or gold. The report shows that of all the central banks of the West, it was the Swiss national bank that regularly presented the largest number of Portuguese notes to the Bank of Portugal.[3]

It is clear that to foreign capitalists, the Swiss banker guarantees both safety and anonymity. He rarely pays any interest worth mentioning on the money received; a federal law of November 1975 requires that a negative interest of 40 per cent per year be levied on exported capital deposited in Switzerland – but don't worry, it is never enforced. The foreign capitalist generally finds the arrangement satisfactory. The Swiss franc has gone up as against the lira, the pound and the French franc by an average of 74 per cent since February 1972. The foreign capitalist does quite well. So does the Swiss banker: with the money he gets for nothing in this way, he finances his own empire, his own multinational companies.

"Switzerland, a garden surrounded by blood . . ." says Nazim Hikmet. In one short chapter it is hardly possible to cover all the contrivances, the pretences, the lies and the complex strategies used by foreign capitalists and their Swiss accomplices to transfer their money into the garden. I will mention just a few.

(1) *Under-invoicing.* A firm – French, Italian, Brazilian, English, Japanese, or whatever – exports goods to country X. The purchase price specified in the contract is ten million, but in fact eighteen million is paid for the goods. The first ten million is paid in the normal way by the buyer, and the seller takes the money home, declaring it to the authorities, and changing it into his own currency which he then banks. The other eight million, however, is paid by the buyer in cash directly into the seller's numbered bank account in Switzerland.

(2) *Compensation.* In Paris, Lyons, Rome, Milan, Madrid and most of the large cities in Asia, America and Africa, there are discreet agencies that specialize in what is called "compensation". They always know exactly what is happening in their country's foreign trade: they follow the flow of goods in and out, how long it takes to get bills paid, fluctuations of currency, and the financial situation (silent reserves, liquidity, etc.) for most of the large companies. Suppose a firm or an individual wants to make a payment in country X: it or he consults one of these agencies, which – often for a very high commission – puts it or him in touch with another client who has credits in that country.

For example: A French importer who lives in Paris is importing machinery from Germany. He proposes to the Bank of France to arrange a perfectly legal compensation with a French exporter working in Germany. But in fact he operates a fictitious compensation (as described in paragraph 1), involving sums far larger than those mentioned in his proposal to the Bank of France. Credits move around, in fact. If importer X has a real debt of 2 million deutschmarks, and creditor Y is owed two million, they may well arrange compensation in Japanese yen or Italian lire, stipulated when payment falls due. The compensation agent who actually effects the currency transaction then speculates on his own account (this is extremely common), or on behalf of one of his clients, on currency fluctuations often involving five or six different currencies at a time; the debt (or the credit) in question thus travels

41

round, from Frankfurt to London, from Tokyo to Paris or New York. The profit that results almost always ends up safely tucked away in a numbered account in Switzerland.

(3) *Renting a safe-deposit box.* This is a very common practice. The foreign capitalist hands over to a network of carriers his gold bullion, jewellery, pictures, furs, or simply his bundles of banknotes. The carrier gets them into Switzerland, hires a safe-deposit box in the basement of a Swiss bank[4] and puts his client's valuables into it. If they are foreign banknotes, of course, the carrier changes them into Swiss francs first. "Founding a bank and robbing a bank are the same," said Bertolt Brecht. He was quite right. The only thing is that banks, finance companies and brokers' offices are being founded all the time in Switzerland; but never in banking memory has a Swiss strongbox been robbed. However there are other, temporary, inconveniences that can threaten carriers and hirers of strong-boxes.

For example: By November 1975, according to the Italian government, the country was losing the equivalent of 55 million dollars a month in exported capital. The Christian Democrat government were wise enough not to threaten legal action against any Swiss bankers. For good reason: most Roman leaders hold large numbered accounts and real estate shares, etc., in Switzerland. (The Vatican is the largest shareholder in the Sidona Bank in Zürich.) The wife of an important Italian politician is co-owner of the Tour de Super-crans, one of the most luxurious winter sports hotels in Europe. But a number of local authorities in Italy, under socialist or communist leadership, decided to put up a fight. They set up a delegation to negotiate directly with Berne. Their message was this: either the Swiss government must take effective steps to stop the outflow of capital (six billion dollars a year), or the local authorities could no longer guarantee the safety of Swiss investments in their respective areas. Those investments are considerable. And there is one peculiar feature about them which became clear in July 1976 with the affair of the Dioxin leak from the Hoffmann-La Roche factory in Seveso, outside Milan: the Swiss multinational companies had transferred to Italy those parts of the production process that might be a danger to the surrounding populace. Hoffmann-La Roche had given up producing Dioxin on Swiss territory (as was stated by the company's managing director, A.W.Jann, in an interview with the newspaper *Der Blick*, in August 1976). The Swiss government were so touched by the anger of this regional delegation that they did something unthinkable: they violated the sacrosanct principle of free convertibility! In April 1976, the Federal Council issued a decree: henceforward, people could change no more than 20,000 Swiss francs' worth of lire or French francs, etc. However, the decree was merely playing to the gallery, for it is evaded every day. A capitalist need only use a larger number of carriers, or, even more simply, he can just hand his money to a private "compensation" agency.

(4) Swiss bankers have discovered another method, which is particularly effective in France, Italy and Spain. A firm practises under-invoicing both at home and abroad, thus making its accounts show a deficit. This has many advantages: the management of the firm has really "solid" arguments for resisting wage demands from the trade unions; they will pay no tax; and in some countries – Italy and in certain cases France – they will actually receive a state subsidy. The whole art then is to keep this "loss-making" firm a few millimetres above the water-line. It must evade *both* bankruptcy *and* profits! How is that done? To keep in business, the "loss-making" entrepreneur will periodically ask for a short-term credits (usually three-monthly). From whom? From the Swiss bank where he keeps his numbered account. The major Swiss banks have subsidiaries in most countries, or if not, they have controlling shares in local ones. But do not these short-term credits cost a great deal? They do. But the monthly interest of 24 or 25 per cent which the businessman needs to pay to keep his plant going are paid to a creditor who looks quite miraculously like the debtor. In short – the lucky fellow is paying himself the handsome profits, for which he at once debits the unfortunate company (limited, or joint-stock, etc.) to which the factory belongs.

B. Dirty money
This falls into two categories. The first is linked with the fact that Switzerland's balance of trade with most of western Europe is in deficit. The flow of illegal capital into Switzerland more or less makes up the difference. If the French government (or the British, or Italian, or German) wanted to take effective steps to stop the loss of tax from their country, and in particular to stop the flight of capital to Switzerland, the Berne government would immediately respond by demanding the re-negotiation of trading contracts. This first category of illegal and concealed funds is astoundingly large: in 1974, the *New York Times* published an enquiry by its editor, Paul Hoffmann, into the town of Lugano.[5] Lugano is the economic capital of the canton of Ticino, an hour and a half from Milan by car; it has 25,000 inhabitants and over three hundred banks, finance

companies, loan companies and stockbrokers. Hoffmann shows that in the period 1964-1974, dirty money from Italy amounting to over 15 billion dollars was deposited in Lugano. All the large Swiss banks (and many foreign ones as well) have branches in Lugano, on a scale quite out of proportion to the modest financial needs of the canton.

As I said, in April 1976 the Federal Council decreed that foreign banknotes could only be changed up to the value of 20,000 Swiss francs. This law is kept in abeyance. Dirty money is managed in the main via international compensation, the under-invoicing of goods delivered abroad, and so on. Let me stress this point by giving another example. A French businessman sends goods abroad. He sells them for 5 million (French) francs, but the invoice officially states three million. The three million is paid by the buyer in his own currency, and put through the Bank of France in the normal way. The remaining two million, on the other hand, is not declared, and goes directly into the French businessman's numbered account in Switzerland.

This under-invoicing of exports will soon involve the French firm in difficulties – but what does that matter? The French taxation system is such that a firm making a loss can get large tax concessions. However, to carry on, the loss-making firm has to get money, by short-term borrowing. From whom? From the Swiss bank where the businessman in question has his numbered account. Consequently, the French entrepreneur will not be paying tax in France, yet thanks to the high interest he pays himself via his Swiss account, he will be making money hand over fist.

According to a recent study, about 400,000 Frenchmen have numbered accounts in Switzerland. Yet there are over a million unemployed in France, and a lot of businesses are in trouble for lack of investment. French wealth in Switzerland is something over 390 billion new francs. According to Jacques Attali, economic adviser to François Mitterand, this represents four months' national production, and at least a tenth of all French financial wealth.[6]

The second category of dirty money comes from the ruling classes of peripheral capitalism.

For example: The Co-ordination Committee of the Ethiopian armed forces who deposed the emperor Haile Selassie on 9 September 1974 were astounded to discover what a vast amount of money he had sent out of the country. On 12 September, Agence France Presse sent on the following communiqué from the committee:

The Committee is publishing the production figures for the gold mines in the south of the country, where a labour force working under duress have, over decades, extracted hundreds of thousands of kilos of gold. That gold was sent abroad for the benefit of the emperor, and one bank even changed the gold into notes, since they no longer knew what to do with so much. . . . The deposits the king made in foreign banks are coded, and there is little chance of being able to use these funds to help the country in its present difficulties. The Committee hopes to arouse enough popular anger to force the king to transfer this money. The first reaction of the average Ethiopian is one of astonishment that such large sums taken from a poor country should be making profits for banks in some of the richest countries in the world. It is thought in Addis Ababa that a large part of this wealth is deposited in Switzerland.[7]

Another example: In 1974, the paper *El Panamá-América* published the following dispatch from its office in Tegucigalpa:

The manager of the Central Bank of Honduras, Porfiro Zavala, says that country is facing a difficult situation because of the export of capital abroad. All those who have exported money have an absolute duty to bring it back again.[8]

The official attributed this situation to the "atmosphere of uncertainty pervading the country, and the present low interest rates". In other words, the timid efforts of the Honduran national government to tax incomes, and thereby to some extent relieve the poverty of the majority of the population, were virtually smashed by the massive transfer of the oligarchy's profits to foreign banks, mainly Swiss, with branches in Panama.

Again from Honduras: on 9 April 1975, *Le Monde* published the following reports:

On Tuesday 8 April on Wall Street, all dealings in United-Brands Company shares were suspended after the company (better known under its former name of United Fruit) admitted having paid out $1,250,000 in bribes to leading figures in Honduras, in exchange for trading advantages.

Time magazine, on 21 April 1975, reported that General Osvaldo Lopez Arellano had received part of this money by way of his numbered account in Switzerland. The list of criminal activities concealed by banking confidentiality is almost endless.[9] I will give one final example:

General Thieu, president of South Vietnam until April 1975, and Marshal Lon Nol, ex-president of the republic of Cambodia, two high-ranking statesmen manufactured by the USA, both gave evidence of having a keen business sense, in addition to their police talents. During the terrible agony of their two peoples, these two philanthropists gave considerable thought to planning their own future. At the end of March a DC-8 belonging to the Swiss Balair Company – a company actually owned by the national Swissair company – landed in Saigon. The plane had been hired by the Red Cross in the German Federal Republic to fly in drugs, powdered milk and medical equipment. It was to depart the following day. But on the morning of the departure, the captain of the aircraft received a surprising visit: two emissaries from the presidential palace in Saigon asked whether his plane could take "some personal belongings" of the Thieu family, and "a few things" of Lon Nol's to Switzerland. What belongings? Sixteen tons of gold, they said. The pilot was amazed and sent a telex to Switzerland. Permission refused. Why? Because, to return to Europe, the DC-8 would have to land twice for re-fuelling, once in Bangkok and once in Bahrein. Balair feared that in one or other of these airports the gold would be seized. This cargo was "too visible": the Swiss were unwilling to take the responsibility, and risk of legal action. Then Saigon had another idea: "Suppose we cut the ingots up into fine strips and conceal them in the hold with another cargo on top of them?" The Swiss again refused.[10] Yet there is detailed evidence to show that that gold – billions of dollars stolen from the people of Cambodia and Vietnam – is today peacefully lying in the vaults of a discreet Swiss bank.

The poor countries have virtually no weapons to prevent their own wealthy classes from sending capital out of the country, for the people doing it tend to be the people in power. Léon Bloy said, "Money is the blood of the poor". This is nowhere truer than in the case of a banking system that amasses wealth untold in the Swiss mausoleums of international finance – out of the surplus-value created by starving people.

In June 1976 there was nervousness in the House of Parliament. With the worsening of the economic crisis in Europe and indeed in the world, a number of foreign governments that had traditionally collaborated with Switzerland (the USA, Germany, Sweden) called for effective measures to be taken against their nationals using the facilities provided by Swiss banks to defraud their own income tax system. The federal government framed a law, which they submitted to Parliament. The law proposed withdrawing banking secrecy from any swindler whose tax evasion should have been established by the enforceable judgment of a properly-constituted court in another country. The great bourgeois press and the political machinery of the right swung into action. Cries and lamentations! What a blow to Swiss sovereignty! On the morning of 21 June, the National Council voted. The socialist spokesmen – Richard Müller, Helmut Hubacher – defended the proposed law. Then came the spokesman of the bourgeois majority, the deputy from St Gall, Rodolphe Schatz. Schatz, naturally, is a banker, a partner in the Banque Wegelin et Cie in St Gall. He spoke, he besought, he intoned, he appealed: the nation was in danger, he cried. What danger? Danger from the foreign investigators of foreign exchequers. Was it for this that thousands of our people fell to defend the soil of Switzerland 650 years ago? Never! Switzerland must be saved – this law must be rejected. Schatz sat down. The federal Finance Minister, Georges-André Chevallaz, stood up. Then the miracle happened: "Schatz is right," he said, "My law is unacceptable; the controversial paragraph must be deleted" (and banking secrecy preserved). And so it was: when the vote was called, 74 deputies voted against, but 91 voted for the strict preservation of secrecy. Swindlers from everywhere, even those condemned by courts in their own countries, could go on cheating the tax-man. They might go to prison at home, but their little hoard would be waiting for them in Switzerland when they came out.

C. Banking secrecy

The admirable Swiss institution that makes all these profitable operations possible – illegal transfers, tax frauds, the complex financing of complex arms and drug dealing, speculation in foodstuffs, international currency fiddles, hiding stolen funds, and all the rest – is called banking secrecy. The legal basis for it is Article 47 of the Federal Law governing banks and savings banks. This is what the article says:

> Anyone who, as member of the banking body, as a bank employee with authority to act, as auditor or liquidator of a bank, as observer on the Banking Commission, or as employee or member of the board of an authorized auditing institution, shall have revealed a secret entrusted to him, or

known to him by reason of his profession or his employment; anyone who shall have incited another to violate professional secrecy, shall be punished by a maximum of six months' imprisonment or a fine of up to 50,000 francs.

If the offence was due solely to negligence, the penalty shall be a fine of not more than 30,000 francs.

Any infringement of secrecy shall be punishable even when the professional service or employment concerned has terminated, or the person in possession of the secret no longer holds the same position.

Exception is made where the provisions of federal and cantonal legislation stipulate an obligation to inform the authorities or to bear witness in a court of law.[11]

There is a long list of those liable to commit indiscretions:

—The members of a body (such as a management board or committee of directors) and private bankers, those associated in any company in an active or a sleeping partnership;
—Agents: this general term covers all those to whom the bank has entrusted any responsibility in the sphere of its commercial activities; the law was particularly intended to include the data centres to which the banks send their information to be electronically processed;
—Liquidators in cases of banks that fail, and likewise the auditors who approve the bankruptcy certificate;
—Experts appointed by the Banking Commission to observe banks whose creditors are in danger of being seriously damaged by major irregularities;
—Those employed in any authorized auditing firm, and also all those on the governing body of such a firm.[12]

In Switzerland, the handling of money has a quasi-sacramental character. Holding money, accepting it, counting it, hoarding it, speculating and receiving, are all activities which, since the first influx of protestant refugees to Geneva in the sixteenth century,[13] have been invested with an almost metaphysical majesty. No words must intervene to sully such lofty activities: everything is done in contemplative silence.[14] Anyone who commits the sin of talking too much desecrates the sanctuary: such sacrilege is punishable by law.

In the Calvinist theory of hoarding as a holy work, this silence and contemplation have a corollary. The banker in Geneva (or Basle or Zürich, or in the Swiss bank in Panama) accepts his function as a staunch guardian of morality: in a world of sinners and unbelievers, his silence keeps virtue secure. Only the honest man benefits from banking secrecy: its anonymity is a reward for his honesty. As the depositary and vigilant guardian of Christian morality, the Genevan banker on principle never lends money to or accepts it from anyone for whose virtue he cannot vouch. *On principle* he only operates inside the area defined by the precepts of the Church and the laws of states.[15]

Unfortunately for him, what he does every day *in reality* is a harsh denial of his principles. A denial, first, in theoretical terms: the Calvinist doctrine whereby accumulating money is a value in itself implies seeing the fact that millions of people are exploited and living a sub-human existence if not as a good thing, at least as an ineluctable historical necessity. This contradiction obviously makes nonsense of the evangelical doctrine of human equality, of the faith and its commandments which the banker is supposedly serving by the institution of secrecy. A denial, too, in practical terms: it is the very fact of secrecy that impels the banker to do the opposite of what he is claiming to do.[16]

D. The practice of the courts

How does one open a bank account in Switzerland? Conversely, how can an account be confiscated? The foreign client who deposits money in one of the four thousand and some banks in Switzerland must show some identity document and give the bank an address to write to. The identity can be fictitious, and the address need be no more than a post-office box number in the Bahamas. (Although the potential client is customarily required to prove his title, in other words to provide evidence of his identity, such evidence is never checked on officially.) There are certain legal obligations whereby, if his client is wanted by the police, the banker must render assistance to the courts. But these obligations usually remain in the realm of theory. It is almost impossible for a complainant, be it a foreign government of an individual, to discover, still less get a Swiss bank to return, money stolen by a third party. To sequestrate a bank account, the complainant usually has to provide the name and identity of the account-holder, the address of the bank, the number of the account, and even the approximate amount of money in it. It is rare for any complainant to have all this information available, and even if he has, his sequestration demand would still probably fail. The procedure – even in an emergency – is to all intents and purposes public, and it only needs a quick telephone call to the bank from the account-holder or his local agent to get the number changed or simply move the money elsewhere.

In parenthesis, I want to make it clear that in my view no blame is to be imputed to our magistrates and prosecutors, who frequently pursue international gangsters and their fences in Geneva or Zürich with an energy and persistence one can only admire. It is the actual judicial processes that let them down. For example: Julio Muñoz, an international financier associated with the family of the dead Dominican dictator Trujillo, became, in the sixties, as so many others have done, an "honest" Swiss banker. He bought the Banque Suisse d'Epargne et de Crédit in St Gall; he founded the Banque Genevoise de Commerce et de Crédit in Geneva. Early in 1973, Muñoz ran into trouble with his international customers, and decided to move to another country – having first removed his spoils. The second bank was made to go "bankrupt": charges were laid in Geneva and Zürich. Muñoz was arrested in Zürich, but let out on a bail of a million Swiss francs; he then disappeared. He was sighted in Spain. Of course Muñoz never answered the summons of the court in Geneva. Time passed, and in April 1975 his swindles virtually received the sanction of the government. There was a question in the Geneva parliament, and the cantonal government replied with disarming candour: "The judicial authorities of Geneva are competent to handle the case; but the whole affair is such an inextricable tangle of the penal with the civil that it would take a *juge d'instruction* and a representative of the public prosecutor a whole year, working full time solely on this case, to unravel it – which is obviously an impossibility".[17] So Muñoz, free, rich and happy, can continue practising his noble profession under other skies.

Endless lawsuits have been going on for over ten years in the Geneva law-courts as the government of the republic of Santo Domingo struggles to recover the stocks of gold and currency "transferred" to Geneva by Trujillo's sons. The sums involved amount to over 500 million dollars. The Geneva legal authorities have been trying in vain to find them since 1965.

Hundreds of Jewish families have sought to recover some of the huge sums deposited in Swiss banks by Jewish firms, communities and individuals during the Nazi period. The banks holding these funds were finally invited by the Confederation to declare *voluntarily* (admirable Calvinist virtue!) all funds "without known owners". Thus the banks had a choice between declaring the money – or keeping it; for the Confederation had no means of enforcing its own law of restitution.[18]

We may consider one last case – a dispute between the Algerian government and the Banque Commerciale Arabe SA in Geneva. The Algerian government wanted to recover FLN funds, amounting to some 50 million Swiss francs[19] (plus interest, accumulating since 1962) deposited in the Banque Commerciale Arabe SA in Geneva by the FLN's treasurer, Mohammed Khidder, in the early sixties. In April 1964, Ben Bella dissolved the political bureau. Aït Hocine replaced Khidder; armed with a mandate from Ben Bella, he went to Geneva to try to withdraw the FLN money. It was no good: Mardam, the manager of the bank, refused to allow Hocine to withdraw funds which, as far as he was concerned, only Khidder could touch. In June 1964, Ben Bella brought an action for abuse of confidentiality in the Geneva courts. After the preliminary enquiry, the case was put on file. Meanwhile, Ben Bella was ousted from power, on 19 June 1965. In the meantime, however, the court had established that the funds had indeed been deposited in the bank in question, and also that, a few days before Hocine arrived in Switzerland, the bank had paid out ten million francs to Khidder. These he had transferred, via a Swiss bank, into West Germany. The total was divided up among several numbered accounts, and the court also discovered that the records of those accounts had vanished. Mardam, the banker, refused to give any details. He was arrested and accused of failing to comply with the demands of the authorities; he was then released again. The investigation followed the usual course. Khidder was murdered by two men (names unknown) in Madrid in 1967. On 2 February 1971, following a fresh civil complaint laid in 1966 by the FLN conjointly with the Algerian government, the high court of Geneva condemned Mardam to pay a fine of 40 million francs. On 13 June 1973, the court of civil justice in Geneva confirmed the judgment. The federal tribunal of Lausanne, the nation's highest court, was finally brought into the case, as court of final appeal.

Both Swiss banks and foreign banks in Switzerland awaited its judgment with some anxiety, for it would establish a precedent. Should not the Swiss banker – or rather, the Syrian banker turned Genevan like so many – have known or been able to discover that an independent government had been ruling in Algeria since 1962, and that Mohammed Khidder, who had been the treasurer of a secret organization up to March 1962, was in 1964 simply a political exile and no longer a representative of the Algerian state? No, said the Judge in charge of reporting to the court. "The banking contract signed when the account was opened made no mention of any representation. Khidder figures in it as the holder of the funds and the only person competent to dispose of them. As far as the bank was concerned, the FLN did not exist. No blame can therefore be attached to it."[20] And the court report adds without a hint of irony: "The federal tribunal unanimously issued this judgment, quite categorically. The plaintiff's counsel did not fail to urge the political and moral aspects of the matter, but our court cared only for the law – in total independence".[21]

Its conclusion was that the Banque Commerciale Arabe SA had no obligation to concern itself with origin of the money. It needed only to know Khidder. But what if the real owner demanded the money back? The federal tribunal did not recognize him. Where was the money? The federal tribunal did not wish to know. Who now holds the 50 million francs subscribed by Algerians working in France? The Banque Commerciale Arabe SA. What happens to the most elementary justice in this case? Banking secrecy is all that matters.[22]

To justify their activity as receivers of stolen goods, the Swiss oligarchy produce a number of arguments. The first – logically irrefutable – I heard in 1974 from a Basle banker in Panama. As far as he was concerned, there was no such thing as dirty money. Switzerland lives by a system of free movement of cash. There is no call for its banks to worry about any national legislation elsewhere that may forbid the export of capital. After all, it is not for the Swiss bank to do the job of the state of Panama. It cannot be expected to scrutinize the provenance of all the money coming into its branches in Central America in the light of foreign national legislation.

The second argument, which is less subtle, I heard on the same trip, repeated endlessly by men in less lofty positions, but with equally strong banking realism: What if Peru decides to nationalize large landed estates or smash industrial monopolies? What if Honduras is trying to bring in the first income tax in its history? It is only natural for the Swiss banks and their agents on the spot to do everything in their power to assist the "threatened" capitalists of Peru and Honduras to evacuate their money.

A third argument is that all this capital is needed to finance Swiss national production inside Switzerland. But the figures suggest the very opposite:[23] the total holdings of all the banks in Switzerland (excluding the finance companies) amounted in December 1973 to about 269 billion Swiss francs. Foreign banks held 29.9 billion of this, or 11.1 per cent. Out of this, 23.8 billion, or 8.8 per cent, was held by banks actually under foreign ownership; and 6.1 billion, or

2.3 per cent, by subsidiaries of foreign banks. The proportion held by the five biggest Swiss banks represented 121.2 billion, or 45.1 per cent. The remaining 43.8 per cent – i.e. 117.9 billion — was divided among another 418 concerns, about 38 per cent of it in cantonal, regional or communal banks. The breakdown of the figures relating to industrial investment, real estate, etc., on the one hand, and to fiduciary money on the other (i.e. money used for activities other than financing production and services in Switzerland), shows that the present needs of the national economy are covered in the main by national savings deposited chiefly in public banks, savings banks, cantonal banks, building societies, etc. The policy of the great merchant banks, as well as the equally active policy of most of the foreign banks, is also totally different: not merely do they handle dirty money from abroad, but they themselves also lend vast sums to be invested abroad.

We can therefore conclude that the Swiss system of banking imperialism is essentially a parasitical one. National savings are adequate to finance national economic expansion. Dirty money from abroad serves not the prosperity of the Swiss people, but the financing of the most risky and the most lucrative undertakings of a tiny oligarchy. In other words, not merely would the destruction of the secondary system of imperialism created by the Swiss banking barons make no noticeable difference to the Swiss economy, but (as we shall see in our concluding chapter) it would mean a new lease of life to tens of millions of men, women and children in the Third World.

E. The reinvestment of the spoils

What happens to the dirty money deposited in Switzerland? Either it becomes a numbered deposit account in Swiss francs, or it goes into "fiduciary accounts". These are accounts in foreign currency held by Swiss banks and used to finance operations in other countries. In theory, then, dirty money passes through Switzerland to be reinvested abroad, where it helps to finance the expansion of the multinational companies whose headquarters are in Switzerland. In practice, anything may happen to it. In fact it would be hard to think of any human activity that is not financed by one or other of the great banks, the ordinary banks, the finance brokers or agencies of Geneva, Zürich, Basle or Lugano. When drug-dealers are caught in America, their Swiss bank accounts figure in their dossiers. The money for the arms traffic in the Middle East and Asia goes by way of Geneva. The "great families" of France stash away their gold in the vaults beneath the rue de la Corraterie. Sheiks from

the Persian Gulf and colonels from Guatemala buy blocks of flats
in Lausanne, Zürich and Geneva : and with the help of their floating

The banking oligarchy do not
deny that they invest some of the
dirty money in the lucrative
markets of Europe and America.
But they insist that part of it
returns to the economies of the
periphery in the form of aid.
What are the facts?
In a developing country the
exchange value of the currency
is not high enough to put it
monetarily on a level with the
industrialized countries. Thus,
for the poor country, repaying a
loan involves the need to pay as
quickly as possible, in foreign
currency, the interest on the loan
– of which the last payment must
be added to the total payment of
the debt when it falls due. In
addition to these normal borrowing conditions, the lending
countries must also consider the
capacity of the borrowing nation
to repay. Credits are granted only
with certain restrictions:
– Creditor nations and multinational organizations reserve the
right to examine the use of credits
destined for specific projects. The
debtor countries seldom have a
free hand when it comes to using
the money lent them.
– The repayment period is
generally too short; the day of
repayment arrives too soon,
before solid results have been
achieved. Hence the (obligatory)
request for a renewal of credit,
and the danger of even heavier

indebtedness.[1]
– Long-term projects, necessary
but non-productive undertakings,
thus seldom benefit from
"development aid". Hanselmann,
the director general of the Union
Bank of Switzerland, makes this
quite clear: "There is one vital
condition for giving credit: the
money must be used for profitable investment, so that it is sure
to pay for itself within a given
time".[2]
It is not hard to work out the
mechanism which turns a debtor
into a still greater debtor.[3]
Suppose an annual loan of 100
million is given, with interest at
8 per cent.[4] In thirteen years, the
interest becomes larger than the
annual credit. The first repayments
probably come in on time. Thus
the developing country must, in
this very short period, have
established an export industry
capable of earning vast amounts
of foreign currency, if it is not
to fall deeper and deeper into
debt.
(from Kappeler, op. cit.)
NOTES
1. W.Guth, Der Kapitalexport, Basle
(Editions Kylos), 1957.
2. NZZ. 28 April 1972.
3. "Problèmes de la dette des pays en
voie de développement", UNCTAD, TD/
118/Suppl. 6/Rev. 1, 1972, pp.32-3.
4. Cf. H.Bachmann, The External
Relations of Less-Developed Countries,
New York (Praeger), 1968, p.7 (tables
showing payment of interests and
dividends, assuring an annual return
of 15 per cent).

capital and the active collusion of certain local property management firms, they can indulge in the wildest property speculation –
to the joy of the Swiss wage-earner who then has to pay the horrific
rents they charge. To this we may add the whole gamut of international stock-exchange investments, loans, trade financing, and
speculating in currency and in foodstuffs. Dirty money is also used
for the complicated but paying operation known as forward buying :
a quantity of foreign currency is purchased for transacting at some

future date. It is not uncommon for capitalists in one country to use their fiduciary accounts for the forward buying of currency from a competitor country, thus weakening the currency of their own country.[24]

I enjoy a morning walk past the glossy façades of the Geneva banks, in the rue de la Corraterie or the rue Petitot. At around eleven, the limousines start arriving – Rolls-Royces, Cadillacs – with number plates from Portugal, Spain, the Lebanon, Greece, or local plates marked with the "Z" that means "foreign". Nationless millionaires step out of them and disappear through the splendid portals. The doorman bows respectfully. The millionaire goes straight up to the second floor, where his Swiss colleague is expecting him. They do their day's work together: they consider how things are moving on the Stock Exchange, and plan their next coup – it could be a massive speculation against the French franc, the liquidation of an industrial company where trade-unionism is becoming too strong, the financial strangulation of a competitor, the financing of an interesting arms deal, or a project to supply cereals to a country where a famine has led to the government's being prepared to pay a high price.

Sometimes the "hyenas", as Brecht calls them, get it wrong, and actually lose some of their money. For example: the *New York Times,* 3 September 1974, reported that the Swiss manager of the foreign exchange department of the Lugano branch of Lloyds Bank International was sacked after causing the bank to lose a trifling 75 million dollars. But this kind of thing is a rare exception. Almost always, the hyenas win; it is peoples and states that lose.

> Tell the man pulling the wagon
> That he will soon be dead.
> Tell him also who will live –
> The passenger inside the wagon.[25]

In point of fact, speculation with dirty money is normally done via local bankers: this gives it a mask of well-bred respectability. Here are a few examples:

In 1975, despite resistance from the bankers, Switzerland had to sign a reciprocal judicial aid agreement with the United States.[26] According to the federal Justice Department in Washington, the American Mafia were tending to transfer their loot to Switzerland, and then reinvest it perfectly legally (by way of fictitious companies and numbered bank accounts) on the New York stock-exchange. (The term "laundering money", coined by the Mafia to describe what is done when illegally acquired assets are put through Swiss banks and then invested quite legally in American companies, has entered the normal vocabulary of the banking world.) It appeared, according to American dealers, that the international drug traffic had also been assisted by the discreet services of certain Swiss bankers.

Voltaire used to say: "If you see a Swiss banker jumping out of a window, jump after him. There's bound to be money in it!" A Swiss private banker can do absolutely anything: there is no end to his skills – merely to describe them would fill an entire book.[27]

The Swiss banking system plays the vital role of receiver of stolen goods for the worldwide imperialist system. But banking secrecy is only one aspect of the machinery that enables it to do so. Two others are significant: "tax agreements", and the system of public supervision of the banks.

When a cosmopolitan millionaire decides to settle in Switzerland, he is in an exceptionally lucky position in relation to tax. A person living on capital is not exercising any lucrative profession in Swiss law; his tax is therefore assessed in terms of his "outward signs" of wealth. If, on the other hand, he still exercises a lucrative profession, if he still "works" from Swiss territory, he can make use of another of the admirable institutions invented by the Swiss: a "tax agreement". This is a contract made between the foreign capitalist and the Swiss tax authorities, which fixes a set sum to be paid every year in tax by the capitalist, thus avoiding the need to have his income assessed by law. Foreign millionaires evading taxation have their regular places to settle in, like migrating birds. They tend to nest around the lakes – Léman, Lugano, Zürich and Maggiore. To name a few of the best-known: Sophia Loren, Audrey Hepburn, Jack Palance, Mel Ferrer, Rex Harrison, Nana Mouskouri, Petula Clark, Steve McQueen, Georges Simenon, Jean-Claude Killy, Gunter Sachs – these birds all nest around Lake Léman. Charles Aznavour, Gilbert Bécaud and Prince Napoleon prefer altitude; they have their nests in Crans-Montana and Pregny. Others – like Baron Thyssen, Hans Habe and ex-King Michael of Romania – drag out their wretched lives on the shores of Lake Maggiore.[28]

To understand how "tax agreements", this special form of international tax avoidance, work, we might look more closely at two examples out of the many; one relates to a European capitalist, the other to a Third World philanthropist. The first: in 1969, the German financier Helmut Horten sold 75 per cent of the shares of his Warenhaus AG, the second largest department-store empire in

Europe. The purchaser, a group of European banks, paid him the modest sum of 875 million deutschmarks. On which Horten did not pay a penny in tax! For he moved house, to Switzerland. Henceforth, he enjoyed the protection of the 1931 German-Swiss double taxation agreement. Had he not moved, he would have been liable to pay the German government around 250 million deutschmarks. A kind-hearted man advised the "refugee" millionaire: Brenno Galli, a lawyer in Lugano, a National Councillor, President of the Swiss National Bank, a personal friend and former colleague of the then federal minister, Nello Celio. With Galli's help, Horten managed to settle in the canton of Ticino, whose legislation does not tax income earned outside the borders of Switzerland. Everyone was delighted – apart from the German tax authorities, and *Der Spiegel*. Public opinion was aroused. Even the Swiss national press, though so perfectly submissive to the higher interests of capital, printed a number of discreet queries. Brenno Galli announced in 1971 that he would not seek re-election to the National Council; but Helmut Horten – happy, rich and at peace – continued to enjoy his fortune in his magnificent estate above Lake Maggiore.

My second example: before 1952, the Patino family ruled the tin mines on the Bolivian Altiplano. Wages there were very low, and Bolivia's infant mortality rate was the highest on the continent. The Patinos made a fortune. They were driven out of Bolivia in 1952, during a popular insurrection. They live today in a quiet village near Geneva: Vandoeuvres. Their money is in Genevan banks. The canton of Geneva, in agreement with the commune of Vandoeuvres, has granted them a "tax agreement" in exchange for their beneficence to the local community (the family had to finance the building of a theatre for the university and a hostel for Latin American students in Geneva).[29]

The system of public supervision of the banks is founded in theory on legislation intended to keep a close watch on their dealings, but this system functions in a rather peculiar way: the banks are by law subject to supervision (the auditing of their accounts) by institutions which are supposed to have no connection with the directors of the bank concerned. But the auditors of the three largest Swiss banks (Swiss Bank Corporation, Crédit Suisse and Union Bank of Switzerland) are not independent at all. In fact, one is controlled conjointly by the first two, and the other by the third! One day, a deputy asked that the Federal Council do something to remedy this, on the grounds that a private auditing firm is in no position to do the job in a fully independent way; supervision ought to be carried out by a public body which should, in addition, be required to keep an eye on the commercial policy of the big banks. At the very least, the private auditors should be supervised by a public body. But the government, faithful to their policy of never doing anything that might cause serious inconvenience to any of the banking empires, refused to intervene. The supervised are therefore still supervising their own supervisors.[30]

1. Lenin's nickname is an unfair one, because it is not the nation but the oligarchy that receives stolen goods.

2. The propaganda services of the banking barons endeavour with great skill to make their receiving operations look like productive activities. An interesting instance of this is an interview with Alfred Schaefer, Manager of the Union Bank of Switzerland, in *Newsweek*, 11 March 1974, entitled: "Our raw material is money".

3. For an analysis of the "Italian" networks, cf. the enquiry of *La Stampa*, Turin, 10 January 1975; for the "North African" networks, cf. *Tribune de Lausanne*, 28 May 1973; for the workings of one of the most powerful "French" networks cf. *Journal 24 heures*, 11 November 1975; and for the "Spanish" network cf. *Der Spiegel*, 19 January 1976.

4. The proliferation of safe-deposit boxes has caused problems in the local politics of Geneva: the banks, like so many moles, are incessantly burrowing under the city – municipal regulations stop them from building any further upwards. They have nowhere to put all the foreign money that keeps flooding in, so they have to keep digging. They are now down to their fifth floor underground in Geneva. If you walk along the rue de la Corraterie, the rue du Rhône, the rue de la Confédération, you are walking on a carpet of gold – mountains of banknotes, securities, jewels, gold and silver. But these Ali Baba's caves present the city with unexpected problems; the concrete casings protecting these interminable corridors with their safes and strong-boxes are now down to the level of the water-table. The banking district of Geneva is on the left bank of the Rhône. The underground water being displaced is destroying the foundations of the buildings alongside the river, so that they have to be condemned. In July 1976, the bulldozers flattened two entire rows of dwellings behind the Quai des Bergues, in the old district of Saint-Gervais. The loss is irreparable. They were houses of great historical interest, the homes of the "cabinottiers", clockmakers who worked at home in long narrow workrooms under the high roofs – the first clockmaking industry in Europe. Jean-Jacques Rousseau and his family lived in one of those houses.

5. *New York Times*, 4 September 1974, p. 59.

6. Jacques Attali, in *Le Monde diplomatique*, May 1976, p.4.

7. The figure given by the armed forces co-ordinating committee was 6 billion US dollars (at the exchange rate of September 1974).

8. *El Panamá-América*, 3 September 1974, p.7.

9. I would say that, in general, the systematic corruption of politicians and administrators in Third World countries by the multinational companies of the centre is part of the regular strategy of imperialism. I mention it here only in relation to the instrumental part played there too by Swiss banking secrecy. For the strategy of systematic corruption, see especially *Corruption in India*, a symposium edited by Suresh Kohli, New Delhi, 1975; also Béchir Ben Yahmed, "La corruption", *Jeune Afrique*, no. 751, 30 May 1975.

10. *Time*, 21 April 1975, p.25.

11. Article 47 of the 1934 federal law on banks and savings banks. There is a commentary on this article and a periodical analysis of the legal position by Maurice Aubert in *Fiches juridiques*, published in Geneva.

12. Aubert, ibid.

13. The wealthy Protestant bourgeoisie of France and Italy flocked to Geneva at the time of the Reformation, and again in 1685 after the revocation of the Edict of Nantes.

14. The architecture of our banks is well designed to convey the sacredness of the activities that take place in them: there are sumptuous temples with

marble colonnades for the big merchant banks, and discreet little chapels with dark woodwork for private banks and brokers.

15. A.Biéler, *La Pensée économique et sociale de Calvin,* Geneva (Georg), 1959; G.Busino, "Intorno al pensiero economico e sociale di Calvino", in *Revista storica svizzera,* no. 10, 1960.

16. We heard a *cri du coeur* from George-André Chevallaz, Minister of Finance, during the parliamentary debate on harbouring funds from Ethiopia (in December 1975): "You can hardly expect a Swiss banker to start questioning a functioning head of state about where he got his money!" It is a serious dilemma indeed: faced with an important client, almost no banker would take the risk – even though it is required by law!

17. Reply from the Geneva Council of State to a question from Jean Vincent in April 1975, transcribed by the *Journal de Genève.*

18. A federal decree of September 1974 closed the file on foreign assets dating back to the Second World War. Two million francs were given away (of the hundreds of millions deposited!) – it was divided among Jewish charities, the Red Cross and the Refugees' aid bureau.

19. This money came from subscriptions paid by Algerian workers in France between 1954 and 1962.

20. *La Suisse,* 2 July 1974.

21. Ibid.

22. In the first edition of this book (Paris, March 1976) I erroneously said that the Khidder family had taken the FLN's 50 million – which they did not. In 1969 they returned all the revelant papers to Algeria, and they later handed over everything further that they managed to recover. Since then, though the tragic death of Khidder himself was a great blow, they have continued to do everything possible to help Algeria regain the money and to make known the facts of the affair.

23. Figures from the 1973 report of the Bulletin of the Association of foreign banks in Switzerland, published in June 1974.

24. For information about the currency dealings operated by Swiss banks with dirty money, see the two appendices to this chapter.

25. Brecht, Poems vol. 7, Paris (L'Arche), 1967.

26. This agreement does not stop the Swiss banks from evading American law; the Crédit Suisse, for instance, refused to submit to the judgement of the Security and Exchange Commission (SEC) which demanded that banking secrecy be waived in regard to certain numbered accounts involved in dubious speculations. Cf. *Weltwoche,* 17 December 1975.

27. I knew and admired Mehdi Ben Barka; he was a powerful thinker, and a tactful and intelligent friend and adviser to the many militants who used to come and visit him at his house at Chambésy (Geneva). However,

28. The last complete list was drawn up in 1972: cf. *Nationalizeitung,* Basle, 21 April 1972.

29. For a comparative analysis of the concessions granted by Switzerland to tax-evaders and those to be found in other tax havens, see A.Vernay, *Les Paradis fiscaux,* Paris (Seuil).

30. Statement by National Councillor Helmut Hubacher, 21 March 1973.

Appendix to Chapter 2

*(Dirty money tends mainly to find its way into two types of
financial circuit: the Euro-markets, and the multinational financial
circuits of Swiss, French and other western industries in the Third
World. Kappeler here discusses the two successively. J.Z.)*

I. Euro-markets

Stocks of dollars are accumulated in Europe which shuttle
around among banks and major companies all over the world. The
sums involved, estimated at 150 to 200 billion dollars,[1] come from
unsecured American loans; they also come from the fortunes of
oil-producers, the vaults of issuing banks, and dirty money from
the Third World.[2] According to UNCTAD, one-fifth of the total
dollars in Europe in 1967 came from the Third World. From 1946
to 1952 it is reckoned that five billion dollars were transferred abroad
by upper-class Latin Americans: this represented 30 per cent of
all the dirty money, and was five times as much as the official aid
received by Latin America during that period.[3] Some experts reckon
that in the early 1960s, capital was exported from Africa and Latin
America at a rate of one billion dollars a year.[4] The proportion of
this that went through Swiss banks must have been considerable. In
1971, a statement by Lutz, general manager of Crédit Suisse, mentioned that between a quarter and a third of the total Euro-dollar
market was handled by Swiss banks.

My own estimation would be that 12 billion francs have come
in from the developing countries – i.e. one-fifth of the 60 billion
francs that constitute Switzerland's contribution to the Euro-dollar
market. But this could easily be an underestimate. Switzerland has
considerably lower interest-rates than those usual on the Euro-dollar
market. Swiss banks pay very little interest (at times none at all) on
dirty money from the Third World. This difference in interest rates
means that their profits are great. Furthermore, in many cases the
banks lend money that has come from the Third World to the giant
enterprises of Europe and North America. Such loans will be short or
medium-term ones, and can take various forms, including direct
loans by individuals to large companies with the bank as the only
intermediary. These are known as "Notes", "Private placements" or
"Certificates of deposit", and are usually for amounts of between
50 and 100 thousand francs. Swiss banks involved large foreign
firms in this way to the tune of over six billion francs in 1971.

Loans of this sort are bound up with the Eurobond market

which the Swiss banks have marked yet more clearly with their imprint. The Eurobond market differs from the regular Euro-dollar market in the length of term of its loans. According to UNCTAD, the dirty money accounted for 80 per cent of investment in the Eurobond market in 1969. As for the investment of such capital in the major Swiss banks, it was thought in 1971 to represent something around half of the total market volume of 3.6 billion dollars.[5] In 1972 that volume rose to 5.6 billion.[6] Given that their share of this capital is in proportion to the overall yield, the Swiss banks handle between 1.8 and 2.8 billion dollars a year from the developing countries on the Eurobond market, to say nothing of the hundreds of millions of francs they collect in commissions, taxes and interest.

In certain of the developing countries, the authorities have set about trying to get back at least some part of these liquid assets. But the only way they do so is by borrowing from that same Eurobond market; and the Swiss and other European banks that handle the ruling classes' exported capital charge a higher rate of interest when the developing countries come to borrow the money back. Latin American countries are charged an interest rate 1 per cent or 2 per cent higher than Europeans and North Americans; African countries up to 4 per cent or 5 per cent higher.[7]

As well as paying interest at this unequal level, there are also commissions, usually amounting to 2.5 per cent of the total sum borrowed (whereas in Wall Street, for instance, it is only 0.875 per cent).[8]

All the dealings in the Euro-market are regulated by the big banks – Swiss, European and American – which have formed into consortia in recent years. Recent creations in which Swiss banks are involved include the European-Brazilian Bank (belonging to the Banco do Brasil, Banque Ameriba, Bank of America, Deutsche Bank and the Union Bank of Switzerland), and the Libra Bank (belonging to the Chase Manhattan Bank, Banco Italiano, Mitsubishi Bank, National Westminster Bank, Royal Bank of Canada, Westdeutsche Landesbank Girozentrale, Banco Espirito Santo and the Société de Banque Suisse). These two organizations concentrate mainly on Euro-market transactions with developing countries. The Swiss Bank Corporation is, for good measure, also tied up with the Banque Americano-Franco-Suisse in Morocco; and the Crédit Suisse became associated with the Bank of Tunisia, and joined with it in 1962 to found a number of banks in West Africa. The geographical distribution of their subsidiaries makes clear how very interesting to Swiss bankers the Third World is. The Swiss Bank Corporation has branches in Beirut, Bogotá, Buenos Aires, Caracas, Guayaquil, Hong Kong, Lima, Mexico, Rio de Janeiro, São Paulo, Singapore and Panama. The Union Bank of Switzerland and the Crédit Suisse follow much the same pattern. Among the most recent developments, we may note that the major Swiss banks have set up issuing houses in the Caribbean and above all in Singapore.[9] The opening of these most recent branches was inspired by the sudden rise of a dollar market in Asia (with a total of 2 billion dollars in 1972).

From all this, four distinct conclusions can be drawn:

1. Powerful markets in dollars and other currencies (florins, pounds) have come into being over the past decade.

2. The ruling classes of the developing countries provide an appallingly high proportion of this capital, which is mainly used to finance projects for trade and industry for the developed countries.

3. Because of the large part played by its three major banks in setting up consortia and in international financing operations, Switzerland draws enormous profits from this wealth. At the same time, though some of this capital is the fruit of tax evasion punishable by imprisonment in other countries, it is quite safe here, because banking secrecy enables the banks to refuse to give information in cases of tax fraud.

4. Creditor-debtor relationships are often multilateral, and subject to no national or international planning or control. They are determined solely by the conditions and interest rates dictated by the business sense of whichever side is economically stronger.

II. Multinational financing of industrial expansion on the periphery

In addition to distributing credits from one country to another, Swiss bankers also share in financing the development of multinational companies. Institutions involved in this include the World Bank, which consists of the IBRD (International Bank for Reconstruction and Development), the IDA (International Development Association) and the IFC (International Finance Corporation). The IDA provides credits on easy economic conditions, and the IFC on tough conditions. There are regional banks for aiding development: the Inter-American Development Bank, the Asian Development Bank and the African Bank. These institutions get their credits by loans, subsidies or borrowings from member countries or donor countries. Switzerland has enabled the World Bank, the Inter-American Bank and the Asian bank to borrow on the Swiss capital market. Switzerland is a shareholder – to the tune of five million dollars – in the Asian Development Bank. Inter-American's borrowings in Switzerland stood at around 250 million francs by the end of 1972, to which must be added loans worth 125 million. Switzerland is the fourth largest supplier of capital to that particular bank. The World Bank borrowed about 1.7 billion francs in Switzerland in 1972: at the end of the previous year even allowing for repayments made, there had still been 215 million dollars to pay back, at an average interest rate of 4.61 per cent.

In 1971, the Asian Development Bank had borrowed 40 million francs at 7 per cent.

In 1972, the Inter-American Development Bank increased the proportion of credits granted on tough conditions (i.e. 8 per cent interest) from 36 per cent to 55 per cent of the total balance. Thus, this institution, whose fourth largest creditor is Switzerland, has taken a major step backwards in the sense of reducing the amount of credit that can properly be called *aid*.[10]

The amount of aid represented by such loans must be virtually nil from the moneylender's point of view. For those who buy into these bonds – mainly small savers, pension funds and large investors – are lending absolutely without risk, and at a slightly better rate of interest than they would get from bonds at home. The banks that act as middlemen charge the World Bank an entry commission at usual Swiss rates – that is somewhere between 1 and 3 per cent of the total value of the loan. Thus, on the 1.7 billion francs the World Bank borrowed in Switzerland, the Swiss banks received commission (entry charges) of between 17 and 51 million francs! Further commission is received when bonds are sold before they actually fall due – since not all buyers keep them for the full fifteen years.

But it is Swiss industry that makes the most from these loans to aid "development". Most of the money lent to the developing countries by the Swiss banks and the World Bank is spent on buying goods in Switzerland. Of the 1.5 billion francs the World Bank had received from Switzerland up to November 1971, 1.3 billion soon came back there (to pay for industrial investment).[11] Five years before that, in 1966, a total of 666 million francs in loans was matched by purchases in Switzerland of as much as 695 million. World Bank interest payments (i.e. indirect payments from developing countries) had already brought an additional 217 million francs into Switzerland.[12]

Notes to Appendix to Chapter 2

1. According to estimates by the Commission pour le Questions de Conjoncture. This should be compared with the supplement to the monthly report of the Banque nationale Suisse, no. 7, 1972. Information given by F.W.Schulthess to the annual general meeting of the Crédit Suisse in 1972.

2. Investments by American firms in 1970 earned 16.8 per cent in Asia (excluding the oil-producing countries), 24.3 per cent in Africa, and 9.5 per cent in Europe. See "US investment rises" in the *Financial Times,* 17 December 1971. If Swiss firms were obliged to publish figures as American firms are, the results would probably be about the same.

3. *The Flow of Financial Resources, Outflow of Financial Resources from Developing Countries,* published by UNCTAD, Geneva, TD/B/C/3, pp.13-14.

4. Fred Hirsch, *Money International,* London (Penguin), 1961, p.244.

5. *The Times,* 6 June 1972.

6. *Financial Times,* 5 March 1973.

7. Ibid., 3 June 1973.

8. Ibid., 4 June 1973.

9. *Die Zeit,* Hamburg, 9 March 1973. Singapore's attractiveness to international capital was emphasized in the Crédit Suisse bulletin of March 1973, which pointed out the great advantage of the low wages paid there by a number of Swiss firms (producing foodstuffs, machinery, optical instruments, clocks and chemicals).

10. *NZZ,* 10 May 1973.

11. Union de banque suisse, *Notes économiques,* November 1971, p.9.

12. *Tribune de Genève,* 31 October 1967.

3
The Chilean Connection

There is an indispensable functional unity linking secondary imperialism to primary. Its non-autonomous, instrumental nature overrides the conflicts among the various imperialisms created by their competitive operations (confrontations at the periphery between the finance capital of two different countries, competition at the centre over the handling of the spoils, etc.). Imperialist activities as a whole are based on a common system of rationality geared to preserving the world system of capitalist domination at all costs (even that of sacrificing an immediately profitable or commercial programme).

In normal circumstances, that is to say when the capitalist order reigns undisputed, this rationality only operates implicitly: it provides a frame of reference for inter-imperialist competition, marking the limits that must not be transgressed by the competitors. But what is now happening more and more often is that subject peoples rebel: they demand freedom and sometimes they obtain it. The world capitalist system can no longer tolerate the development of liberation movements like those begun in Africa in 1960 by Lumumba, or in Latin America in 1956 by Castro. The days of "imprudent" or "liberal" imperialism would appear to be past. At the slightest hint of a bid for freedom by a subject people, a multi-form repression is set in motion. Secondary imperialisms have a vital role to play in this initial crushing operation, for in many cases, the primary imperialism and its political expresson – the US government – cannot intervene directly and openly for reasons of global political strategy. The primary imperialism then appeals to the capitalist rationality that underpins the world system of domination, and the first defence of the threatened system is entrusted to one or other of the regional sub-imperialisms. For example: suppose a popular rebellion takes place in Dhofar, and threatens the imperialist bridgehead of Oman? The Iranian armed forces will be ordered to crush the popular movement. Or suppose an anti-imperialist government is established in La Paz? Then the Brazilian secret services will engineer the fall of Torres and bring in Banzer.

When a country gradually liberates itself within its own previous constitutional framework, by voting in a popular government, then the situation is peculiarly difficult. All that imperialism can then do is to crush these impudent people economically and financially. That is what happened in Chile. In the slow and methodical process of strangling the people of Chile, the secondary imperialisms of Europe – the leading non-American associates of the Chilean economy – played a decisive part. Switzerland especially. From the moment President Salvador Allende took office in November 1970, the United States and its European allies organized systematic sabotage of and interference with the Chilean economy.[2] The international coordination of the scheme was effected by the "40 Committee" in Washington, chaired by Henry Kissinger.[3] Gerald Ford summed up far better than I could the underlying rationale of this inter-imperialist operation:[4]

> Question: Under what international law do we have a right to attempt to de-stabilize the constitutionally elected government of another country?
> Answer: I am not going to pass judgment on whether it is permitted or authorized under international law. It is a recognized fact that, historically as well as presently, such actions are taken in the best interest of the countries involved.

What of Swiss secondary imperialism? It would be absurd to think of a hot-line between the 40 Committee in Washington and the headquarters of the banking empires of Zürich and Geneva. The underlying rationale of the imperialist system operates virtually of its own accord. The specific motivation behind the repressive function of secondary imperialism was clearly stated in March 1973: in reply to a question from me, the Federal Minister of the Economy, M. Ernest Brugger said this:

> Normal dealings are no longer possible with Chile . . . We have our economic system, and the Chileans have preferred to opt for a different one. That is their privilege, but let no one try to tell me that we should be pleased by their choice! I may not have a great political brain, like the questioner, but I am a grocer and a businessman.[5]

The crushing of Allende's Chile, that "silent Vietnam" as he himself called it, was a complex affair. It would require a longer book than this to analyse it. All I can do here is look at just a few of the measures taken by the secondary oligarchy of Switzerland, in collusion with the oligarchies of other imperialisms, to suppress Chilean democracy.

Controlling as they did certain key-sectors of the Chilean economy – such as foodstuffs – all the Swiss imperialists had to do to cause the new government virtually insurmountable difficulties was to refuse to collaborate with it. For example: Nestlé controlled almost the entire production of tinned dairy products and instant coffee, as well as a large proportion of all other Chilean tinned food. The company had been in Chile for over thirty years. Its subsidiary, Chiprodal SA, controlled six factories, in the following localities: Graneros (tinned milk, Nescafé and derivatives), Los Angeles and Osorno (tinned milk), Llanquihe (powdered milk), San Fernando (Maggi products – soups and stock-cubes, etc.) and Rancagua (pasteurized milk). The other Nestlé subsidiary, Savory, made ice cream and frozen foods (Findus) in Santiago. With these two subsidiaries and their seven factories, then, Nestlé effectively dominated the Chilean market. The production policy and price structure of Chiprodal and Savory had always been geared to satisfy primarily the needs of the Chilean upper classes. The innumerable poor families in the shanty-towns and settlements and mining centres of the north and the migrant workers of the south were almost never able to buy any of the tinned baby-foods or condensed milk produced under the Swiss patent. For all the thirty years of Nestlé's presence in Chile, therefore, hundreds of thousands of Chilean children were as badly off as ever. Their growth stunted for lack of protein, many grew up as invalids. The Popular Unity government wanted to put a stop to this situation, and decided to distribute a half-litre of milk a day to every needy child in the country up to the age of fourteen. To do this, the Allende government needed to negotiate with the Nestlé trust, to have some kind of control over the company's pricing policy – especially over the cost of milk. Nestlé would not agree to negotiate in any form.[6]

I remember an afternoon in April 1972 – the southern autumn – in Santiago. We were together on the veranda of "Tomas Moro", the modest white house where President Allende lived. Seated in a high-backed colonial-style armchair, his dog at his feet, Salvador Allende talked about his youth, about his early experiences as a young doctor in a suburb of Valparaiso. He would never forget the undernourished children he saw there, he said. That was why he had given up his comfortable job for the insecurity and, at that time, apparent hopelessness, of battling as a socialist militant. Now he had come to grips with his enemy and was looking him straight in the eye. History is a funny thing: the rebellious young doctor who had raged impotently against institutionalized malnutrition was now head of state, leader of a revolution. At this stage, he had not yet admitted defeat in his battle with Nestlé. He was questioning me with passionate interest – or rather, with that amused curiosity which could suddenly turn to passion in mid-sentence – about the characteristics, the way of life, the ideological background of Villars, the managing director of Chiprodal, and about Corthésy and other top people in Nestlé-Alimentana in Vevey.

As the sun was going down, and I was about to leave Tomas Moro, Allende suddenly said: "If you want to know about the Chilean revolution, go to Nueva Habana tomorrow morning. The milk trucks will be arriving around ten". So, the following morning, I stationed myself at the stated time in the main (dirt) road of the Nueva Habana shanty town, opposite the kindergarten run by the young women of the MIR. Within a short time, three grey trucks arrived, jolting along the bumpy surface left by the rain. They were surrounded from the moment they entered the shanty-town by a mass of joyful children and mothers, and a few workers on holiday. The milk had been bought with precious foreign currency in Argentina. As long as I live I shall never forget the looks on those children's faces as the drums were unloaded.

Switzerland is the home – in fact that is one of its main functions within the worldwide capitalist system – of the headquarters outside America of a great many of primary imperialism's companies. Anaconda and ITT, two multinationals whose role in the international campaign to sabotage the Chilean economy is well known,[7] operated from Switzerland. A large number of other, less well-known companies acting from Swiss territory also played clearly-defined roles in the strangulation of Allende's Chile.

Internordia Finanz SA is one of many holding companies to have its headquarters in the canton of Glarus for tax reasons. Shortly after coming into office, the Popular Unity government arrested seven people for economic sabotage. The Chilean Senate gave the case several hearings. During one enquiry session, Senator Narciso Irureta stated that Internordia had caused the Chilean state a loss of several million dollars. Among the seven accused was Alfred König, a director of Internordia. The affair led to a crisis in the company: Werner Stauffacher, vice-president of the management board, resigned in protest against the activities of his own company.[8] According to the enquiry, Internordia Finanz SA, of Glarus, attempted to buy a million tonnes of copper at a very low price. The operation was rendered easier – according to the same Chilean Senate enquiry – by the fact that corrupt Chilean officials were skilfully concocting totally false reports on the prospects of selling Chilean copper once Popular Unity were in power.[9]

To turn to a third level: it was probably the banking empires of New York, Zürich and Geneva that played the most important part in the destruction of democracy in Chile. It was there that the co-ordination of repressive measures by primary and secondary imperialism was at its most effective.[10] The starting signal was given in August 1971, a few months after the nationalization of the copper mines. The Export and Import Bank of Washington refused the Chilean aviation company, Lan Chile, a loan of 21 million dollars to buy three Boeing transport planes. This was odd because Lan Chile is a model borrower, paying its debts on time, and the loan was intended, as previous loans had been, for the purchase of American planes in the USA.[11] Gradually the noose was tightened, as one by one the various sources of credit were cut off. By the end of 1972, Allende's Chile was totally isolated. Then there began the sinister series of campaigns to sabotage the economy. The engineers' strike in the Teniente copper mine in 1973 lasted seventy-four days and cost around 75 million dollars (in terms of lost foreign currency). A series of lorry-drivers' "strikes" damaged the Chilean economy badly – for in this 4,000-kilometre-long country, almost all domestic transport is by road. The last of these "strikes" cost Chile about 6 million dollars a day in spoiled foodstuffs (meat, vegetables and milk). Sabotage campaigns like these could not have lasted and spread had they not been supported by foreign financiers. I will outline the way it worked, as described in the Italian paper, *Il Manifesto*.

This paper published[12] a study of the Banque pour le Commerce Continental, whose headquarters is in Geneva (15 quai des Bergues). It is owned by a Chilean family called Klein which belongs to the right wing of the Christian democrats. During 1972 and 1973, a number of right-wing Chileans came to Geneva to meet with Klein and various other bankers. Even Frei was seen in Geneva with the Kleins, in February, March and July 1972, and again in January 1973. Orlando Saenz, president of the Sociedad de Fomento Fabril, was in Switzerland very shortly before the coup to drum up support among his friends in banking circles. Saenz is a considerable figure on the extreme Right in Chile, and belongs to the fascist movement "Patria y Libertad". He is now economic adviser to the Junta.[13] Starting in January 1973, two million dollars came into Chile in small denominations ($10 at the largest). In August 1973, when inflation was in full swing, vast quantities of dollars were circulating in Santiago. The first to benefit from them were the truck drivers on

71

"strike" against the Allende government. One man in Santiago admitted that he and his colleagues were given 7 dollars for every day they were on strike: on the black market this fetched 10,000 escudos, at a time when the normal monthly wage of a lorry driver was only 40,000.[14]

On 11 September 1973, the fascist officers and American special services brought Chilean democracy to a violent end. The multinationals returned in triumph, with the consequence that by June 1976, two million Chilean children were suffering from serious malnutrition, half of them being likely to die of starvation.[15] How did the official government of Switzerland react to the re-establishment of the colonial régime? Despite the protocol that requires all flags to be flown at half-mast when a head of state dies in office, the bourgeois majority in the Federal Council refused to lower the flags on any public buildings; unlike the governments of most of the civilized countries, the bourgeois majority in the Federal Council refused to send a condolence telegram to the widow of the murdered President; and, in Santiago, the Swiss ambassador, Charles Masset, shut down his embassy when the putsch began and refused asylum to the dozens of refugees who asked for help.[16] Finally, on 23 February 1974, the bourgeois majority in the Federal Council decreed that refugees from Chile must have entry visas to come to Switzerland – which was effectively saying that (with very few exceptions) they were not to come at all. This inevitably recalls an extremely nasty precedent: on 17 October 1939, the Federal Council decreed that German Jews must have visas to enter the country – thus implicitly handing over men, women and children to their Nazi executioners.[17]

Notes to Chapter 3

1. Complementing the function of repression there is also one of reinforcement: secondary imperialism works as a vital instrument in repressing popular, reformist or revolutionary governments on the periphery, and at the same time assumes a function of furthering oppressive régimes which are useful to the strategy of the centre (such as Indonesia, Brazil or South Korea). In this chapter we have been looking at the repressive function of secondary imperialism, with reference to one particular case, that of Chile under Popular Unity (1970-73). However, in the two appendices to this chapter, the reinforcing function appears alongside the repressive one. They look at the way the government uses the two main weapons of repression and reinforcement – the federal export risk guarantee, and bi-national or multinational aid to developing countries.

2. A.Uribe, *Le Livre noir de l'intervention américaine au Chili,* Paris (Seuil), 1974; see also A.Touraine, *Vie et Mort du Chili populaire,* Paris (Seuil), 1973; J.C.Buhrer, *Allende, un itinéraire san détours,* (L'Age d'homme), 1974.

3. For the activities of the 40 Committee, see the *New York Times,* 8 September 1974, pp.1 and 26.

4. White House press conference, reported in *Time,* 30 September 1974, p.16.

5. From the shorthand report of the National Council, Spring session 1973, Chambres fédérales, p.156.

6. The Swiss chemical industry is well represented in Chile. Ciba-Geigy, Sandoz and Productos Farmacéuticos Roches hold a privileged position in the health business. Bührle-Oerlikon, which makes armaments, and is today one of the fascist junta's largest suppliers, controls four plants in the mechanical and construction industry via its subsidiary in Panama (Finsura). In this latter sphere, Sika and Brown Boveri are also very powerful. Cf. *L'Industrie suisse au Chili,* Berne (Group Suisse/Tiers Monde), November 1973.

7. *Multinational Corporations and United States Foreign Policy, Hearings before the Committee on Foreign Relations, US Senate, 39th Congress, The International Telephone and Telegraph Company and Chile 1970-1971,* Washington (US Printing Office), 1973, 2 vols.

8. See *NZZ* no. 143, 26 March 1971; *National Zeitung,* 28 March 1971; also the documentation "Suisse-Chili", in *L'Industrie suisse au Chili,* p. 10.

9. A new light was cast on this affair by the statements of William Colby, the former CIA official: "The CIA infiltrated Chilean agents into the upper echelons of the Socialist Party. Provocateurs were paid to make deliberate mistakes in their jobs", *Time,* 30 September 1974, p.21.

10. Colby maintained that the necessary moneys had been brought in via Europe.

11. *Time,* which recounted the whole story, said that "the airline had a perfect repayment record", 20 September 1973, p.17.

12. *Il Manifesto,* 3 October 1973.

13. Other Chilean fascists had their careers made by the coup. For example: Herrera Gonzales, a police general dismissed by the democratic government, was appointed ambassador to Berne. By an irony of fate, he found his former "boss" Nathanael Davis in Switzerland: this philanthropist was Kissinger's special envoy to Santiago during the preparation of the putsch, and has been US ambassador in Berne since 1975.

14. Cf. *New York Times,* 8 September 1974, p.26.

15. Cf. *Der Spiegel,* June 1976.

16. Under pressure from public opinion, the conduct of the Minister for

Foreign Affairs and his ambassador gradually improved afterwards. In November, an official from the federal ministry finally went to Santiago to select two hundred lucky Latin American exiles and persecuted Chileans considered "worthy" of asylum in Switzerland.

17. E.Bonjour, *Histoire de la neutralité suisse,* Neuchâtel (Baconnière), 1971, vol. vi, pp.10ff.

Appendix to Chapter 3

*(Of the various weapons used by secondary imperialism to prevent
social, economic and political reforms in a subject state on the
periphery – or, alternatively, to reinforce the repressive and anti-
popular behaviour of such states – two are particularly effective: the
federal guaranteeing of export risks, and the international credits
known as "financial aid". Hollenstein analyses the first in Part I,
and Kappeler the second in Part II. J.Z.)*

I. The guaranteeing of export risks

The state gives all exporters who do business with the developing countries a guarantee for whatever credits they export. The
guaranteeing of export risks (GER)[1] insures the exporter against
all risks (currency, transport, political fluctuation) and against the
insolvency of official borrowers. Export credits and the GER put
the Swiss export industry into a very favourable position vis-à-vis
its competitors, giving it an extra attraction at the expense of the
developing countries whose exporters enjoy no such support and can
never therefore be on an equal footing. On the other hand, the
exorbitant cost of export credit – interest at the going market rate,
brief terms of repayment, only the briefest periods of grace – forces
them into buying from their creditors, which involves the developing
countries in additional expenses amounting to at least 20 per cent
of the competitive price level. Obviously, then, this form of financing increases the heavy debt of the states on the receiving end, whose
economic and political dependence on the industrial states is thereby
intensified. . . .[2] In 1970, the Swiss government declared a reduction
of the guarantee rate to 75 per cent – with a corresponding increase
in the risks of exporting. This step was supplemented by a directive
to the GER commission, which said among other things: "When
considering a request for a guarantee, be especially careful about
the conditions for payment."[3] The results have been ambiguous:
there have been instances of guarantee rates being as low as 50 per
cent, but almost every request has been granted.[4]

The GER commission has no precise criteria for dealing with
the more negative effects of export credits. To keep the debt within
acceptable limits money must only be lent to the extent that the
investment being financed brings back (or saves) as much currency
as is needed to repay the loan with interest. Since it is virtually
impossible to work this out with certainty in every case, the only
practicable course is to establish a ceiling for each country – accord-

ing to its stage of development and how deeply in debt it is already – expressed as a percentage of the total capital allotted for export credits. But this has not so transformed the GER as to make it part of a policy of aid for development. There are too many injustices still for that, and the structure of world trade, operating as it does to the disadvantage of the developing countries, has barely been changed at all. Export credits are still expensive, and represent a financial instrument for suppressing freedom.

To look upon GER merely as a kind of insurance must fundamentally hamper aid to development: this can be recognized clearly in the case of Allende's Chile – the only country whose régime met with disapproval. Credit exported to Chile was no longer guaranteed for longer than six months. The policy of the Allende government, trying to achieve basic social reforms and long-term development, was thwarted by sabotage from abroad (credits were blocked by the USA, by the World Bank, by the IBRD; copper prices were manipulated by the USA; and so on), and from the upper class at home (who stopped investing, sent their capital out of the country, etc.). Chile was thus tied up in the most enormous financial problems. Every political reform of course brings its own problems soon enough; and I certainly would not deny that Allende made mistakes, but they were insignificant compared with sabotage from other countries. In particular, the reforms planned included the nationalization of key foreign-owned industries; the interests of various foreign economies, among them the Swiss, were affected. By the terms of the GER, the government would have to pay compensation. From a business-insurance point of view, then, it was quite justifiable to stop guaranteeing credits exported to Chile. From the standpoint of a policy of aiding development, the obvious course would have been to support the Chilean experiment by returning a 100 per cent guarantee, or better still, by freely-given financial backing. The political dimension of the GER, strenuously denied by the Federal Council – "The GER will never be used for political purposes; it is solely and simply a business matter"[5] – can be clearly seen in the case of Chile. To stop guaranteeing export credits without giving any financial aid instead was equivalent to issuing a serious reprimand, indeed a total condemnation, of Allende's policy. During that same period, repressive and authoritarian states like Indonesia found it quite easy to get foreign capital (both aid and investment) and were not subject to any pressure from outside: there was no need to withhold credits. The GRE joyfully took part in this "development strategy" which, underpinned by the interests of private capital, could only reinforce under-development. And, to the extent that the compensation paid exceeded the premiums paid for credit export guarantees, this policy of helping private interests was also financed by the Swiss taxpayer (Hollenstein, *op. cit.*).

II. International credits described as "financial aid"

In international export/import trading, goods nowadays are increasingly delivered on credit. But to save the exporting firm from having to bear the cost of this itself, a bank acts as go-between between exporter and importer. It pays the exporter the sum of the sale price, and gives the importer in the other country a medium-term credit (i.e. one to five years). This combination, advantageous in itself, enables an importing country to buy the goods it needs even if it cannot pay for them immediately. For the exporting country, export loans become a major sales weapon on the world markets. For the developing countries, this sort of borrowing to pay for imports is, at first sight, very advantageous. However, if the use of this "facility" is prolonged, the problems (described earlier) arising out of dependence on foreign capital become evident; the burden of interest increases, and payment dates loom nearer on the horizon. "The money owed by the developing countries has reached an astronomical figure: at present it adds up to over 60 billion dollars. This involves the hidden danger that the capital flowing into the developing countries from the industrialized nations cannot be used for productive purposes, because most of it has to flow straight back as loan repayment and interest".[6]

This trend was evident in the figures for Swiss export credits in 1970: further loans were given to the tune of 97 million francs, while 250 million came back into the country from the Third World in *interest* (not repayments, just interest) on earlier loans.[7]

As I have said, the guaranteeing of export credit is a facility for the rich countries. The major Swiss banks will, for instance, use the money they get from the sale of bank bonds – mainly from small savers – to finance these credits. In 1972, this amounted to 23 billion francs for the 72 largest Swiss banks. The banks only have to pay $5-5\frac{1}{2}$ per cent interest on this, whereas they get around $7\frac{1}{2}$ per cent for export credits. Thus, on the 2,336 million francs of export credits guaranteed by the GER, they get over 40 million francs a year (1970 figures) from the developing countries. This means even more profit for the export trade, while the underdeveloped countries remain hungry, impeded by their incapacity to export.

The underdeveloped countries have grasped the fact that they can play the "delivering" countries off against one another, since they are in competition for the export of credits. This competition among exporters makes for a continuing improvement in credit terms, and ever lengthening periods for repayment. But the developed countries have soon discovered their own community of interest. As long ago as the fifties, they associated to form the Berner Union, in which they agreed not to provide export guarantees for transactions in which the period for repayment was more than five years.[8]

In the summer of 1972, the OECD, as the organization of the richest countries in the world, did all it could to restrain such competition as still existed. From then on, no credits must be exported for a period longer than 5 years without previous consultation and exchange of information. Switzerland was a party to this agreement.[9] No developing country would henceforth be able to play one industrial country off against another. Quite the reverse: the developing countries can now be told by the Swiss that they may find themselves in competition with one another. "The Latin American countries must realize that, in their search for foreign capital, they will be competing with Asia, Africa and Australia, and that those with capital to lend will be guided in their choice by a nation's solvency, profitability and future prospects".[10]

Export credits are always given with a purpose; in other words, they are always intended to finance a specific project. The developing country receives credit from Switzerland when making a purchase in Switzerland. The industries or banks involved can thus impose cumulative conditions. Credits transferred under government auspices are used almost solely to finance exports from Swiss industry. The developing countries, in using the credits granted by Swiss banks and the government, are therefore dependent on Swiss manufacturers as regards delivery dates, choice of products, and prices.

The credit given to India is an example of this. In the middle sixties, on the initiative of a Swiss industrial trust, an outline agreement was concluded between Switzerland and India, for a credit of 100 million francs. The credit was made available by a group of Swiss banks, and insured by a federal export risk guarantee (GER). It was earmarked to pay for the export of Swiss goods. Statements were made about "new forms of Swiss aid to development", and it seemed that the interests of Swiss exporters would be served along with those of Indian importers. A year and a half later, we read in the papers that only a tiny number of purchasing contracts approved by the authorities had been formally concluded between the two parties. The reason is clear: the credit was opened at a boom period, when Swiss export firms could not produce enough to keep up with the demand or fulfil their obligations; they had to turn down further orders. So, suddenly they reduced their collaboration in "aid to development". Credit without strings attached would have been far more to the point in the circumstances. India would then have been free to spend the money inside her own borders, or in some other country.[11]

When credit agreements of this kind are made, it is likely that Swiss industry makes clear what will suit it best to provide. In 1964, the Federal Council produced a report on a credit agreement made with Pakistan:

> The agreement with Pakistan is based on a combination of government export risk guarantees and credit made available by private business. Pakistan will get more of the investment goods it needs from Switzerland, and our industry will be able to play a larger part than before in assisting development projects in Pakistan. The agreement will not prejudice the possibility of ordinary conditions of payment for deliveries of investment products.

Later on, in 1967, the loan rose from 43 million francs to 63 million, for the purchase in Switzerland of broadcasting equipment, textile machinery and electrical plant.

Of the 20 million Swiss francs in credits granted by Switzerland to Colombia in 1968 (other funds were supplied by the World Bank), the Federal Council's eighty-first report on economic activities abroad pointed out that "This credit enabled the Swiss electromechanical industry to secure a 12 million franc share in the execution of the project".

Credit conditions prevailing between Switzerland and the Third World are a reflection of the relationship between the two parts of our world: on the one hand we see the poor nations, with very little chance of stimulating their economies by using finance credit to assist their own exports; on the other we see Switzerland, which pays cash on the nail for its imports and can buy wherever it wishes; it can offer its banking capital to the developing countries in the absolute certainty that the money will come back in the form of purchases of investment products. It will return a second time, later on, in the form of interest payments (say 8 per cent over fifteen years), and a third time as repayment of the loan. (Kappeler, *op. cit.*)

79

Notes to Appendix to Chapter 3

1. Except when otherwise stated, this information comes from the *Loi fédérale sur la garantie du risque à l'exportation,* and the subsequent regulations for its implementation.

2. In 1968, such credits represented no more than a quarter of the foreign debt of the developing countries, yet they accounted for half the cost of debt servicing (L.B.Pearson *et al., Pearson Report,* p.188).

3. Cf. the report: "La garantie contre les risques à l'exportation de la Confédération en 1969", Berne, 1970, p.3.

4. Information given by the President of the GRE commission.

5. Federal Councillor Brugger, when the 86th Report of the Federal Council to the Federal Assembly was being debated in the National Council, said this when describing economic activities abroad and other matters of foreign policy in reply to a question from the author, National Councillor Jean Ziegler, about the consolidation of the Chilean debt (National Council Proceedings, 13 March 1973).

6. B.Fritsch, *Tages Anzelger.* 13 January 1973.

7. R.H.Strahm, *Industrieländer-Entwicklungsländer,* Nurnberg (Laetare), 1972, p.111.

8. H.Brunner, "Die Berner Union und ihre Ziele", *Der Volkwirt,* supplement to no. 45, 7 November 1959.

9. *NZZ,* 16 June 1972.

10. J.Hanselmann, general manager of the Union Bank of Switzerland, to the Latin American Chamber of Commerce, *NZZ,* 28 April 1972.

11. U.Brogle, *Zur Frage des schweizerischen Kapitalexports,* Zürich (Polygraphischer Verlag), 1963, pp.68-9.

II

The Violence of Symbols

4
"Swiss Democracy"

And there are two languages, above and below
And two standards for measuring
And that which wears a human face
No longer knows itself. . . .

But those who are down below are kept below
So that the ones above may stay up there.

Bertolt Brecht
Saint Joan of the Stockyards

Because it is non-autonomous and only instrumental, our
secondary imperialism has an advantage : its activity is almost totally
masked by a pacifist ideology that is never challenged. It would be
hard to convince a Vietnamese peasant recently bombarded by the
US Air Force, or a Chilean or Bolivian prisoner tortured by CIA
experts, of the peaceful, humanitarian and philanthropic character
of American foreign policy. However, he has no trouble believing
in "Swiss neutrality". How has this myth managed to achieve such
extraordinary permanence? The answer is complicated : we have to
find it at several different levels of activity.

We must ask first : how has a nation that has inherited one
of the richest democratic traditions of Europe let itself be robbed
of its inheritance and come instead to be implicitly in alliance with
the sorry ideology of amassing capital, of the "necessary" exploitation of dependent human beings, and the maximization of financial
profit? The answer must be that that ideology is never expressed so
bluntly. In other words, "Swiss democracy", which is the institutional framework in which the imperialist oligarchy functions in
Switzerland, is in reality based on rather different ideological foundations.

The symbolic violence operating at every level of education,
discourse and information, has brought into being a prevailing
ideology from which few Swiss people, however intelligent, are
immune.[1] Its significance extends beyond the political system to
include a whole set of values and images personified by this nation
of equal, likeminded, virtuous, hard-working and just citizens.

Let us take a look, then, at the elements that go to make up
our Swiss "democracy" :

Switzerland is the land of *secrecy*. The commercial bourgeoisie show a remarkable capacity for concealing their own activi-

ties. They can also make a moral or patriotic virtue out of the means of concealment they use. For example: banking secrecy, which represents professional discretion and respect for the rights of others, is linked with neutrality to form a typically Swiss whole – durable, practical, efficient and highly moral; it enables the Swiss oligarchy to make vast profits out of any armed conflict that occurs, in Europe or on the periphery. There are no complete statistics of Switzerland's wealth; statistics of industrial production have stopped being published; no detailed statistics of private Swiss investment abroad have ever been compiled; similarly, when money is deposited in Swiss banks, the federal bureau of statistics does not happen to want to enquire into its ownership or its origins.

In the second place, Switzerland is the land of the *consensus*. The nature of that consensus is complex. To take an instance: Switzerland enjoys a régime of "industrial peace", resulting from an agreement concluded between the employers and the steel unions in 1937. Faced with the menace of Hitler, the two sides swore eternal harmony; strikes were henceforth to be submitted to arbitration – which means that they virtually disappeared. So skilful are the oligarchy that they have since managed not merely to extend this agreement to almost every sector of production, but to keep it in force by tacit renewal to this very day. Between 1937 and 1974, there were only three major strikes in Switzerland. Until the recession in 1975, the working class remained totally demobilized – i.e. for over thirty-five years.

The reasons for this lack of organization are primarily subjective: the prevailing ideology, put forward by the oligarchy and the employers, affects every aspect of life, and appeals to the finest moral values. In fact it stimulates all that is best in the character of Swiss workers, technologists, peasants and civil servants: their pleasure in work well done, their undisputed technical skill, their industrial creativity, their sense of responsibility and initiative, their enthusiasm for work, and their unfailing care with tools and machinery. The prevailing ideology sets a high value on all these capabilities and virtues, and then goes on to use them to its own advantage.

Fraud becomes objectively possible inasmuch as the oligarchy, the owners of the great banks and multinationals, have amassed such colossal wealth both inside and outside the country that they can afford to give some of it away. In other words, thanks to an extraordinary accumulation of capital – derived not only from the super-profits gained from human labour and banking surplus inside the country, but also and above all from the dirty money deposited with them by oligarchies all over the world – the banking barons are in a position to pay relatively high wages to their local employees.[2]

The accumulation of finance capital and the high level of domestic production, while guaranteeing the maintenance of monopoly profits, also provide enough surplus to ensure that even the least powerful citizens have a comparatively decent standard of living: there is poverty in Switzerland, but it is only residual.

There are other basic reasons for this consensus: Switzerland, whose present structure is very similar to some of the multiracial national states of Africa, is an intensely "tribalized" country. Its collective life is essentially lived within the framework of highly compartmentalized communes, regions and cantons. The history of Swiss institutions is one of the slow and difficult integration (still not completed) of communities differing ethnically, linguistically, religiously and socially. Being from the Valais or the Vaud is generally more significant than being working-class. Which means that, as long as there is full employment, workers will feel they have more in common with their Valaisan or Vaudois employers than with fellow-workers from other parts of Switzerland.

One conclusion, then, might be that this consensus, actually an artefact of the great multinational employers and their former allies, the local bourgeoisies,[3] has become identified in the minds of workers, technicians, peasants and government employees with the Swiss character, the essence of being Swiss. In other words, the consensus operates in such a fashion as to make it almost impossible to attack it.

Swiss "democracy", however, is also founded on a declared *respect for differences of opinion*. Quite a paradox! One would have thought that unlimited pluralism would exclude the existence of a régime based on unanimous agreement – and vice-versa. In fact, of course, this pluralism of opinions is not unlimited: it is strictly regulated. Only such opinions, ideas, statements and actions as do not bring into question the structures on which the system (and therefore the predominant power of the oligarchy) rests are held to be "democratic". All other views, whatever their motivation, are declared "contrary to democracy". There is, of course, fierce opposition to the system within that regulated terrain, but to the extent that such opposition really opposes and threatens the non-egalitarian, oligarchic foundations of the system, it is firmly condemned and repressed.

The assumption that confidentiality and secret dealing are

moral virtues, that consensus equals patriotic national unity, and that declaring respect for all opinions guarantees equality: these are the three ideological tools of Swiss democracy. In other words, the liberal bourgeoisie – whose hard core, the finance oligarchy, wields the weapons of symbolic violence – has created a system of *unanimism* and *pseudo-equality*. But obviously the system cannot conceal all the inequalities that exist. When it fails, the liberal bourgeoisie – like everyone who has ever confected an ideology designed to mask a system of exploitation – have recourse to what they call "the logic of things". In other words, they naturalize the problem and say it is beyond their control: Switzerland, the country of the consensus, of secrecy, of repressive unanimity and spurious equality, is also subject to the so-called "natural" laws of economics, and more generally of human history. Since God or nature distribute their blessings unevenly, we are bound to find the Turkish or Spanish sub-proletariat living in hovels, while leisured millionaires enjoy life in their villas in Cologny (an enclave of the financial oligarchy, on the left bank of Lake Léman). It is natural, it is inevitable, it is just "how things are", that tax legislation, the system of symbols and the distribution pattern of political and economic power should bear harder on the former, while making things easier for the latter. At best, the bourgeois liberal believes, and convinces others, that the inequality that bears so hard on the Turk or Spaniard will be remedied as the effects of economic growth in the future permit. Thus, the system presents a double choice to the poor Swiss citizen or the exploited foreign worker: [4] a man can believe himself equal to anyone because, in theory, it is a system in which all are the same (with respect for individual liberty and a politics of consensus), or he can blame his real inequality on some supposed natural process, some ineluctable economic logic, or even on God – which really boils down to the same thing. [5]

The way in which the ruling class – in this case the directors of the transnational banking and industrial companies – and their allies explain to themselves what they are doing is obviously no sort of scientific theory. If it were, it would make it impossible for them to continue doing it, for any real examination would make them see how their activities work, whom they benefit, whom they exploit, whom they kill, whose eyes they are pulling wool over. The whole thing would grind to a halt. The reverse is what happens: the ruling class produce explanations that give a totally false picture of what they are doing, so that they can carry on as before, secure in the belief that their activities are logical, innocent, natural, inevitable, helpful to the nation and the community. The ideology that the ruling class impose on those they dominate does not deceive them alone: it frequently mystifies its authors as well. Indeed it is quite common to find leading exponents of imperialism who genuinely believe in the benevolence of their own mission. Furthermore, the barons of multinational industry and banking make lavish use of those ideologies of the past which have been implanted in our minds by all of our education and social training as universal truths, upon which to base our criteria for judging reality. What is really being done by the ruling class, the class who represent imperialism, is therefore judged to be *right* by the standards of a *false* ideology.

I have several times used the concept of symbolic violence, which is a very useful one in trying to understand how the secondary oligarchy manipulate people's minds by way of their ideology. It is time to look more closely at this concept. Bourdieu gives a convincing basic definition: "Any power of symbolic violence, any power, that is, that succeeds in imposing its own meanings, and imposing them as legitimate by disguising the relationship of force upon which its strength is based, is adding its own strength to that relationship of force."[6] The weapons, instruments and tools operating at the symbolic level are seen as analogous with those that operate at the physical level for the same purposes of domination. Like the physical weapons of domination, these symbolic weapons too have their history, their institutions, their custodians. Among the most vigilant of those custodians are schools, the press and the mass media.[7]

The Swiss Confederation is a living body scarred by wounds from the past. Its history is one of the most exciting and turbulent in Europe. When we think of that history, we are compelled to ask again: how can the ruling political class, i.e. the electoral bureaucracies in charge of its internal debates, manage against all reason to preserve this concordat-based régime of spurious consensus and pseudo-equality?

Since they achieved political and economic power around the middle of the nineteenth century, the capitalist and commercial oligarchy of Switzerland, whose core is the imperialist oligarchy, have never been fundamentally challenged.[8] The French bourgeoisie were shown in their true light at Vichy, but the social history of Switzerland has never seen any comparable breakdown. Unless they ares driven to it, oligarchies never impose their symbols explicitly. They are simply taken for granted.[9] To all appearances, the symbolic violence functions of its own accord. The oligarchy have certain unspoken declarations available to serve their strategy. These rest upon the way all the social and cultural institutions actually function in our country today – the most effective being undoubtedly education and language. The Swiss oligarchy have never found themselves obliged to explain in so many words how they operate. Only those opposed to the system have to do any explaining. All the tactical decisions of the oligarchy (and their mercenary force – the state) follow from an *implicit* strategy.

I will give an instance of exactly what I mean. I was at dinner at the Swiss embassy in Bogotá in 1971. The ambassador, Etienne Serra, an intelligent and not particularly conventional man, had invited the leaders of the "Swiss colony" – a revealing term, is it not? – to dine with him that day. There was a lively and pugnacious Basque, the general manager of Nestlé in Colombia, a smart young German-speaking Swiss who was the Colombian representative of the Union Bank of Switzerland and President of the Swiss School, and a number of philanthropists busy making their fortune at the expense of the Colombian people. There were others at the table – the distinguished governor of Bogotá and his pretty and amusing wife, an elderly senator, and so on. The subject under discussion was the Andean Pact. The agreement that had just been signed among the Andean nations stipulated in particular that not more than 14 per cent of the (annual, pegged) profits made in any of the Andean Pact countries could henceforth be sent back to Europe or North America. Neither patent royalties nor, *a fortiori*, undeclared transfers of funds (made by means of fraudulent invoicing) were included in this figure. But oh, the outrage! The protests! Honour impugned! All the weapons from the arsenal of hypocrisy were brought out that evening: "Switzerland must not be damaged", "Switzerland would never agree", "After all Switzerland has done for your poor country", etc. What was curious was that it was the *foreign* directors of multinational companies registered in Switzerland who were fiercest in their defence of the Confederation's interests. At no point was it possible to distinguish between the two totally different points at issue. At one level, the most obvious, was the fact that a bank or industry operating from Zürich or Vevey – by the rational decision of a sovereign state, Colombia – could find itself restricted in any way in the transfer of the enormous profits it made year after year; at the other, less obvious level, was the question of where the hypothetical interest of the Confederation really lay, since one of its avowed aims was to promote the independent development of the exploited countries.

Such was – such still is – the power of symbolic violence, that throughout that long evening, I never managed at any stage to get any of those present to admit that the interest of Nestlé or the Union de Banque Suisse was not necessarily identical with the collective interest of the people of Switzerland – or indeed that, candidly, the whole past history of our country proved that the two interests were in point of fact antagonistic. I was wasting my time. It is impossible to argue with a director of Nestlé-Colombia about either his choice of investments (strategic choices) or his pricing policy (tactical choices), for the symbolic system of the political society with which he identifies himself (Switzerland) assumes that the maximization of individual profit is, if not the highest good, at least a "natural" economic law.

Here is another example: it illustrates the confusion so skilfully created by the ideological machinations of the Swiss merchant banks between the financial strategy of the banking empires and the country where (for tax reasons) they have their headquarters. On 24 June 1974, *Time* magazine carried a full-page advertisement: "More Swiss than Swiss: Crédit Suisse, your Swiss bank".[10] This sort of thing is not merely nonsense: it is humiliating for any Swiss citizen who finds himself being thus associated against his will with a commercial exploitation he despises. In New York, in the heart of Manhattan (Fifth Avenue at 49th Street) stands Swiss Centre. A single vast office houses the services of Swissair, the Swiss tourist office – and the Société de Banque Suisse. A single, vast neon sign (SWISSAIR/SWISS TOURIST OFFICE/SWISS BANK CORPORATION) projects into the New York night the lying message that there is an identity of interests and plans between the banking empire and the Swiss state. In its advertising in the American press, the Swiss Bank Corporation also does the same thing. Its favourite slogan reads: "Swiss, Swiss Bank, Swiss Bank Corporation", and this is printed above a picture of two caricatured Swiss citizens, deep in thought. There is a federal law against the unauthorized use of the name Switzerland, or of the Swiss coat-of-arms, but the government never enforces it. In short, between the durability and internal consistency of the collective super-ego and its extreme potential violence, it today assists more than one dominant ideology with the weapons of symbolic violence: this is the true "Swiss mentality".[11]

So, let us look again at symbolic violence: the essential activity of any system of symbolic violence is to prevent the conditions that would enable any real opposition to come into being. "As long as what I write says nothing about authority, or religion, or morals, or the powers that be . . . or anyone who owns anything, I can print what I like – it need only be inspected by two or three censors", says Beaumarchais's Figaro. His tirade is echoed in the plaint of a really conservative writer, Gonzague de Reynold, from his château in Fribourg: "I know from experience what risks there are in wanting to say freely what one thinks in this free country."[12] Reynold and Beaumarchais put into bitter and ironic words just what it is that the Swiss political class mean by two harmless-sounding terms – "positive criticism" and "negative criticism". Positive criticism is fine: it describes any argument that is restricted to forms and subjects determined beforehand by the established order: in other words, it is allowed for by the system. On the other hand, anyone who does not stop at merely ritual opposition but goes on to attack one of the institutions or activities whose preservation is vital for the imperialist oligarchy to wield real power autocratically – is anathema. Their power is supported by an unspoken taboo.

A deputy who violates that taboo comes up against subtle social repression in various forms: he is first accused of failing to be "serious", or of being too "extreme" in his judgements. The régime soon starts trying to discredit him personally, by means of sedulously sustained calumnies, of organized defamation. This, for example, is what happened to Arthur Villard, a socialist and pacifist member of the National Council.

Hundreds of Swiss men and women (to say nothing of political refugees and foreign workers) – some well-known, some anonymous, some courageous over a lifetime, some only in a momentary surge of boldness – have found, and are still finding day by day, just what it costs in Switzerland to express "negative criticism" or to act upon it.

Notes to Chapter 4

1. Marx rightly spoke of the "tragi-comedy" of this bourgeois republic that imagined itself "to be as independent of the class struggle as of the European revolution". Cf. Marx-Engels, *Collected Works,* vol. 8, p.246, London, 1977.

2. There are none the less deplorable inequalities in Switzerland. For example: the 541 richest taxpayers in the canton of Zürich, i.e. 0.1 per cent of the canton's population, own a net wealth of 6.92 billion francs, or 20.31 per cent of all the money in the canton. The wealthiest 10 per cent of taxpayers own 28.3 billion, or 82.61 per cent of the canton's money. Consequently, the remaining 90 per cent own 5.94 billion among them, or 17.30 per cent of the money in the canton. (Figures for 1969; cf. *Maldéveloppement: Suisse/Monde,* 1975).

3. For the conflict arising between the multinational bosses and the local bourgeoisie see Part IV, *infra,* "First know your enemy".

4. For systematic discrimination against immigrant workers in Switzerland, see the appendix to Part II.

5. For a detailed analysis of the social function of Christian belief and the use made of it by the banking oligarchy, cf. H.Luthy, *La Banque protestante en France,* 2 vols, published by the Ecole pratique des hautes études, 1959. See too M.Weber, *Die Protestantische Ethik und der Geist des Kapitalismus,* Archiv für Sozial-Wissenschaft, 1904-5; and the same author's *Gesammelte Aufsätze zur Religionsoziologie,* Tübingen, 1921.

6. P.Bourdieu and J.C.Passeron, *La Reproduction, éléments pour une théorie du système d'enseignement,* Paris (Minuit), 1970, p.18. See also A.Petitat, in *Cahiers Vilfredo Pareto,* no. 25, 1971. Bourdieu and Passeron have produced three other works which help to identify various aspects of the concept of symbolic violence: Bourdieu, Passeron and Saint-Martin, "Rapport pédagogique et communication", *Cahiers du centre de sociologie européenne,* 1965; Bourdieu and Passeron, *Les Héritiers,* Paris (Minuit), 1964; Bourdieu, Passeron and Chambordon, *Le Métier de sociologue,* Paris, Mouton, 1968.

7. P.Bourdieu, "Le marché des biens symboliques", *Année sociologique,* 1971.

8. What is even more disturbing is that people outside the country usually confirm this state of affairs by unquestioningly reproducing the distorted picture of Switzerland presented to them by the oligarchy. Though there are exceptions, French writings about Switzerland give ample evidence of this.

9. For instance, the view of relations between different cultures: cf. R.Preiswerk and D.Perrot, *Ethnocentrisme et Histoire,* Paris (Anthropos), 1975.

10. Obviously Switzerland is not the only country where this happens. To quote Marx: "From the first, the great banks decorated with national titles were merely associations of private speculators, who took up their stand by the side of governments", *Capital,* part 7, chapter XXIV, 6 (Everyman edition).

11. I am convinced that this "mentality" can only be understood with the help of the key concept of the class struggle as applied both nationally and internationally. Hence my disagreement with such serious and well-documented books as J.F.Aubert, *Précis constitutionnel de la Suisse,* Berne (Franke), 1974; G.A.Chevallaz, *La Suisse ou le Sommeil du juste,* Paris (Payot), 1967; A.Siegfried, *La Suisse, démocratie-témoin,* Neuchâtel, 4th edition (Baconnière), 1969; J. Rohr, *La Suisse contemporaine* (A.Colin), 1972; G.Sauser-Hall, *Guide politique de la Suisse,* Paris (Payot), 1965. Of more critical works I would specially suggest P.Secrétan, *Plaidoyer pour une*

autre Suisse, Lausanne (Age d'homme), 1973; H.Tschäni, *Profil de la Suisse,* Lausanne (Spes), 1968; D. de Rougemont, *La Suisse, Histoire d'un peuple heureux,* Paris (Hachette), 1965; L.Boltanski, *Le Bonheur suisse,* Paris (Minuit), 1966.
12. Gonzague de Reynold, preface to *Billet à ces Messieurs de Berne,* Neuchâtel (Baconnière), 1939.

5
Lying as a Holy Duty

PEACHUM :
To be a good man – what a nice idea !
But there's the little problem of subsistence :
Supplies are scarce and human beings base.
Who would not like a peaceable existence?
But this old world is not that kind of place.

Bertolt Brecht
The Threepenny Opera

Things are never simple. There is a subtle dialectic at work between the realms of the normal and the pathological. Obeying the rules is not just the opposite of "deviance" : the two are interlinked in a complex and continually shifting relationship of contradiction. In Switzerland, the enemy is first and foremost the troublemaker, the intruder who interrupts the ceremony, the miscreant who suddenly tears away the veil so that the reality that was meant to be concealed is laid bare. Serge Golowin, an original writer and a deputy in the cantonal parliament of Berne, says: "The enemy is the anabaptist, the man who stands up in the city square of Münster in Westphalia, and tells the powerful to their faces that they are sinners and that the world will come to an end".[1] He can be tolerated so long as he appears at a regular time and in his permitted place, and so long as he too utters the ritual words his audience expect to hear. But the moment he starts trying to get inside the institutions, trying to gain access to those who make the decisions, showing signs of doing the unexpected and escaping from society's control, then he becomes quite simply a danger, and will be burned like Münzer.[2]

Yet, paradoxically, in their heart of hearts, the powerful know quite well that they are sinners. However safe, however tried and tested the machinery for getting away and hiding the incriminating evidence that their consciences have built over years of activity, they would be ashamed to admit, some among the merchant bankers and arms dealers – and the politicians who protect them – are well aware that hundreds of children die as a result of their activities every week, in Bolivia and Ethiopia and Bangladesh. All they can do is to look at the anabaptist from a *fideist* point of view.

Fideism is a word used by Thomas Aquinas to indicate belief in ideas that are accepted as true but which are, at the same time, recognized as impossible by the mind receiving, assimilating

93

and ratifying them.[3] Any qualitative opposition to the federal consensus is seen by the imperialist oligarchy, and the electoral bureaucracies they finance, as a direct threat – not only to their political aims but to their very existence. Hence, all the negative values of official society are attached to such opposition. It is rejected out of hand. But below the level of conscious perception, certain odd mutations can be seen: the condemned protester is the bearer of a message that sows doubt. Suppose that, after all, fundamentally, *in abstracto,* outside the realm of actual possibility, that protester were right? Out of such a split comes a *fideist* perception.

I will give some examples. The first two relate to my parliamentary experience, while the third shows the working of fideist perception in the bourgeois-dominated press.

First example: Berne, on a dull November morning, in 1969. I am in the office of Nello Celio, a lively, jovial, forceful little man, federal councillor and Minister of Finance. His office is decorated with contemporary sculptures, and our interview is due to last fifteen minutes. In fact I stay for three and a half hours. We have an exciting discussion about the statement I am preparing to make in Parliament on preventing capital being exported to Switzerland by the oligarchies of the dependent countries.[4] Celio absolutely agrees with me. The problem of dirty money, of the life-blood flowing from the poor peoples into our Swiss banks, is of deep concern to him. He sees it as a major cause of destitution, hunger and death for multitudes living precariously on the periphery of the industrial world. "You will accept my statement, then?" I ask. "No. I believe in it of course, but the same money would only go to Monaco or the Bahamas instead!" Needless to say, my statement was rejected both by the Federal Council and by Parliament.[5]

Second example: The racist régime of South Africa represents a policy and a view of man diametrically opposed to the convictions of almost the entire population of Switzerland. Yet Switzerland is the second largest foreign investor there. Direct investment by Swiss trading, industrial and finance companies in South Africa rose from 100 million Swiss francs in 1956 to 1,300 million in 1971. South Africa's borrowings of Swiss francs on the international capital market by 1976 had amounted to 2,265 billion Swiss francs. Exports which in 1962 stood at 102 million francs, had risen by 1972 to 330 million. Eighty per cent of the gold sold by South Africa on the open market passes through Zürich.[6]

There was a tremendous uproar in Parliament in 1968. The United Nations held an International Conference on the Rights of

Man in Teheran, at which Switzerland was represented by Ambassador Auguste Lindt, a remarkable man who had formerly been the UN high commissioner for refugees. He made a courageous speech in which he said, among other things: "The Swiss people condemn the policy of apartheid as practised in South Africa." This aroused a storm at home: National Councillor Paul Eisenring accused the ambassador of having exceeded his instructions, and demanded that the government dissociate itself from him.[7] Luckily, the Minister for Foreign Affairs found the perfect answer: to support South African apartheid was totally contrary to the wishes and convictions of the Swiss people, but the federal government ought not to disturb the good relations existing between Switzerland and South Africa – for the simple reason that, "If Switzerland does not finance South Africa, someone else will be bound to!"

Third example: the *Neue Zürcher Zeitung* is the most authentic voice of hegemonic capital in Switzerland. Given that capital's dominant position in various parts of the world, the *NZZ* has a certain international prestige in right-wing business circles. And it must be added that, in terms of the message it seeks to convey, the paper is extremely competently produced.[8] Here is an illustration of the way the *NZZ* processes the news. In 1972, there was a scandal that went round the world press. The multinational company, Alusuisse, with the help of Australian speculators, was in the process of driving some aboriginal families off their ancestral land in the Australian outback.[9] The land contained bauxite. The World Council of Churches, and a great many other secular and religious groups in England, Australia and Switzerland spoke out against what was going on. Alusuisse was supported by an intensive newspaper campaign, led by the *NZZ*. Its argument ran thus: the aborigines are perfectly happy, and this industrial development will make them even happier; it is just that the Left in Europe wants to make people believe otherwise. Alusuisse completed its project successfully. Then a year later, 27 May 1973, the same paper published a page and a quarter of intelligent and detailed analysis, illustrated by large and most moving photographs, of the poverty of the aborigines and how they are exploited by Australian and foreign big business. This article[10] is the best analysis of the subject to have appeared in the European press to date. The two complementary events – the arrival of Alusuisse and the dispossession of the natives – were both reported with scrupulous precision. However, the paper firmly refused to recognize any causal relationship between the two.

The oligarchic régime that still governs Switzerland with all the trappings of republicanism rules, then, by symbolic violence. That is to say, the oligarchy acts in disguise. But can its disguise resist the assaults of reality? Cracks are beginning to appear in it today. My own view is that as compared with the smug arrogance of the ruling ideology, fideism represents a step forward. The rich and powerful are still following their path of arrogance, but their step is more hesitant, stumbling, less assured. The advance of the class struggle and the anti-imperialist struggle, with the clash of ideologies that these struggles involve, are helping to show up the contradictions and lies of the ruling ideology for what they are. Such clashes represent a counter-violence that we must do our best to develop. When I say that fideism represents a step forward, I mean that it represents the Swiss oligarchy's last hope of explaining what they are doing rationally, within the framework of the consensus system. But, as we have seen from a number of examples drawn from the most diverse levels of the oligarchy's social activity, the fideist endeavour is now also nearing the point of collapse. Inconsistency can go no further. All that remains for the secondary Swiss imperialist oligarchy is to turn to a neo-fascist ideology and/or a technological-management ideology that rejects the interposition of any moral values at all and is therefore a lot more savage.

Notes to Chapter 5

1. Interview with Serge Golowin, 1973.
2. Thomas Münzer, the Anabaptists' leader, was beheaded in 1525: cf.
E.Bloch, *Thomas Münzer als Theologe der Revolution,* Frankfurt
(Suhrkamp), 1964.
3. For an analysis of Thomas Aquinas's thought, cf. Marie D. Chenu, *St
Thomas d'Aquin et la Théologie,* Paris (Seuil), 1963.
4. J.Ziegler, *Dépôts bancaires provenant des pays en voie développement,*
Statement no. 178/10328, National Council.
5. National Council proceedings, 30 September 1970, pp.240ff.
6. Figures from *Suisse-Afrique du Sud,* a publication of the Centre Suisse/
Tiers Monde, Geneva 1973. On the massive emigration of Swiss technologists
to South Africa, Namibia and Rhodesia, cf. *Les Nouveaux Mercénaires,*
published by the Anti-Apartheid Movement, Geneva, 1975.
7. National Council proceedings, 13 June 1968.
8. Marcel Beck, professor of Swiss history at Zürich University, has said:
"The *NZZ* exercises censorship by the way it classifies the news" (*Der Spiegel,*
1975).
9. Since 1969, Alusuisse has had a 70 per cent interest in the "Joint Venture
Gove" – a project for extracting bauxite in Northern Australia. In its first
phase, the consortium was to produce 500,000 tonnes of alumina a year.
This would then be converted into aluminium in the group's various plants
in Europe, Iceland, the United States and South Africa. In the next phase
production was to be doubled. All in all, 1.5 billion Swiss francs were
invested. Alusuisse has a 50 per cent interest in the Nabalco company which
was in charge of the Gove scheme, and undertook to develop 8,000 square
kilometres of forest land in the area. Now in 1931, that land had been
established as a "reservation" for the Yirrkala people who had been living
there for at least a thousand years. Without even consulting them, the
Australian government granted the Australo-Swiss group a twenty-five-year
concession. The Yirrkalas sued Nabalco and the government, for flouting
the rights they had been given to the land in 1931. But they lost their case.
The reason given was that *living* on land is not enough to give people a right
to it: the land must also be *improved* (i.e. developed by capitalist production
methods). Cf. documentation compiled by the World Council of Churches,
Geneva, 1972.
10. E.Haubold, "Die Not der schwarzen Australier", *NZZ,* no. 242, foreign
edition, 27 May 1973, pp.5-6.

6
The Colonization of
the Domestic Political Rulers

"Liberal democracy is the form of government used by the bourgeoisie when they are not afraid; when they are afraid, it is fascism," said Ernesto Che Guevara. At present, the Swiss bourgeoisie are not afraid. In principle, the Swiss confederation, and the twenty-two states or cantons of which it now consists, are organized on the liberal democratic model.[1]

The word "liberal" designates a specific phase in the history of constitutional ideas in Europe: the constitutions of most of the Swiss states or cantons date from the mid-nineteenth century; they express the ideology of the new industrial, banking and trading bourgeoisie of that time who, under a cloak of religious wars and ideological conflicts, and with the support of popular uprisings born of social conflict, drove out the old patrician oligarchy – a class already weakened by the Napoleonic occupation and by their own internal contradictions. The period of the class struggle that ended with the victory of the capitalist comprador bourgeoisie more or less began with the withdrawal of the French occupying troops from Geneva in 1814 (Geneva being liberated by confederate troops), and concluded with the acceptance by the people and the majority of the member-states of the second federal constitution of 1874.

Before we analyse the institutions of the visible government and their colonization by the oligarchy, let us take a look at the political forces underlying the institutional system. The Swiss Confederation is governed by an alliance of political parties whose history, social origins and ideology in most cases go back a long way. However, none of these parties represents a "unified social movement", in the sense understood by Alain Touraine.[2] Our parties are essentially national federations of local and cantonal parties or organisations, loosely linked together. Those parties – apart from the Socialist Party and the "Labour Party" (the Swiss communists) – are basically bureaucracies that have been grafted on to the electoral system and speak the now ritualized language of the social struggles waged in the nineteenth century and the first thirty years of the twentieth. The Socialist Party and the Labour Party, whose history is bound up with that of the workers' movement and the workers' International, are still the vehicle of expression of the social struggle and the moving force for any possible popular mobilization, despite the bureaucratic tendencies of some sectors of their organization. Other communist and socialist groups, such as the (trotskyist) Marxist-Leninist League, the (maoist) Marxist-Leninist Party, Progressistische Organisationen de Schweiz (POCH), and the Independent Socialist Party of Ticino, have considerable influence and following among the young.

The coalition at present represented in the Federal Council and in control of the Federal Assembly comprises Christian Democrats, Radicals, Social Democrats and Agrarians (known as the Centre Union). There are 29 parties in Switzerland altogether. Some three million men and women have the vote, and only 10 per cent of them belong to a party. Only 10 of the 29 parties are national; of those only 6 wield any real influence nationally, and only three have members in all of the 22 cantons.

There is no party with an overall majority. Each of the three main parties – Christian Democrats, Radicals and Social Democrats – regularly gets about 20 per cent of the votes in national elections. Their capacity to mobilize the people is virtually nil. All over the country, statutory general assemblies organized by the parties bring together groups of fifty or a hundred, sometimes even two hundred. Apart from a few tired people, no one today seems to want to turn out to listen to a political speech in a school playground. The proportion of people voting in plebiscites keeps going down: up to 1972, the abstention record was 67.2 per cent – a record established in 1919, when only 32.8 per cent of the electorate bothered to vote on temporary arrangements for elections to the National Council and the Federal Council. However, this record was beaten in June 1972 when there was a plebiscite on two decrees: despite their importance (one dealt with building, and the other on the currency) only 25.8 per cent of the electorate troubled to vote.

To understand the present state of the official political forces in Switzerland, one must go back a bit. The Confederation had one very short period of being organized in a democratic and egalitarian way: this was from the founding alliance in 1291 – when the peasant communities of the central Alpine valleys of Uri, Schwyz and Unterwald combined to resist Austrian colonial domination on the passes, particularly the St Gothard – until the rise of the urban business classes in the middle of the fourteenth century. Having concluded the founding pact in August 1291, the peasant communities in the valleys organized a guerrilla war. The chateaux, fortified buildings and defences of the Habsburgs' agents, built in the valleys along-side the roads to the passes, were burnt down. In 1302, one of the rebel peasants, supposedly called William Tell, killed the most famous of all the foreign governors, Gessler, as much for political reasons as in defence of his own family. This was the origin of the myth that helped to produce nationalist literature in the nineteenth century: "Power is at the end of a crossbow"; "The only landlord is the free farmer on his own land", etc. In 1315, the emperor sent an expeditionary force. The Austrian army, equipped with the most modern weaponry (a vanguard of cavalry in armour, con-tingents of cross-bow and long-bow archers) appeared at the north-ern end of Lake Aegeri, to put down the revolt in the valleys. Near the hamlet of Morgarten, a narrow pass where, for about a kilo-metre, the road runs between swamps on one side and steep wooded cliffs on the other, the rebels waited – men, women and children. The Austrian army came on: they were crushed by tree-trunks, blocks of stone, flaming torches flung down from the cliffs above. The survivors were finished off with scythes and thrown into the swamps. Until the coming of Napoleon, no foreign army again pene-trated the valleys.

Safe in the ensuing peace, the new ruling classes established themselves. Local aristocracies set themselves up with the primitive accumulation of commercial capital made possible by their control of the Alpine routes from north to south. They did little in the way of local investment. The valleys remained extremely poor, and there were terrible famines. To resolve the problems of over-population in this infertile land (where there was no public spending to im-prove agriculture), the heads of the ruling families thought up an ingenious solution: they sold their compatriots to foreign govern-ments.

The mercenary system was the result of a number of different causes: it was primarily a source of profit made possible by the chronic unemployment or under-employment of a large part of the population of the countryside. It was also a means of social advance-ment for the mercenary himself (and whoever could compel his services), since his labour was greatly valued on the international market. But the system can only be understood in terms of feudal society. The feudal system made it possible for subjects to be con-scripted; hiring one's subjects out to a foreign sovereign made it possible, not only to make considerable financial profits, but also to form prestigious alliances with powerful rulers. In other words, the mercenary system was the principal instrument of foreign policy for the ruling classes in the old Confederation. The "superfluous" sons of poor families in the mountains of central Switzerland went away and died fighting to defend the interests of French kings, Italian dukes, German emperors, and most of all of the Sovereign Pontiff in Rome (especially when the Papal treasures were pillaged in 1527). Around the end of the eighteenth century, 70,000 men from the confederated states and subject territories of Switzerland were a permanent element in foreign armies. Eighty generals sold these men to the highest bidder and to assist in the most immoral wars. Here is one example of the class relationships to be found within mercenary regiments:

> On 31 August 1790, the Lullin de Châteauvieux regiment, commanded by a Genevan officer, but mainly recruited in the Vaud area, mutinied at Nancy. The rising was not strictly speaking political; its chief cause was that the men's wages were late. But the cantons saw it as a stain on the honour of the Swiss name; the war council of the Castella (Fribourg) and Vigier (Soleure) regiments were all the more ruthless because these were conscripts from a subject territory. They determined to make a terrifying example of them. One of the ringleaders was broken on the wheel, 22 were hanged, 41 were sent to royal galleys at Toulon, and the rest banished from the Confederation forever.[3]

This semi-voluntary deportation of superfluous peasants did not merely bring a lot of money back to the ruling families, but also enabled them to take part in the complex machinations of international politics with skill and profit. In the meantime, the Confederation of the three original valleys had become larger. New states, territorial federations of peasant communities, bishoprics or fortified cities, had joined the alliance. Following a series of territorial conflicts, bargainings and external threats, the Confederation of three had become between 1315 and 1400 a Confederation of eight; then between 1401 and 1516 five more states joined it. However it suffered a blow in 1515 when the Swiss mercenary army was routed by the French at Marignano.

It was not by a voluntary decision that the Confederation abandoned its aggressive foreign policy, but because of a lengthy period of internal upheaval. Four years after Marignano, an unknown chaplain who had been with the Swiss forces in Lombardy set out to preach the Reformation in Zürich. His name was Ulrich Zwingli – and the powerful city-state of Zürich was converted to the new religion. Berne followed. The Reformation, marking the destruction of theocratic feudalism by the urban middle classes with casual help from the poor peasants, made progress and spread all over Europe. In 1536, Geneva expelled its Prince-Bishop and proclaimed itself a republic; it was there that Calvin established his Reform. A skilled statesman, he turned his new protestant allies in the Swiss Confederation against his neighbouring enemy, Savoy. The General of the Bernese armies, Hans Franz Nageli, invaded the Catholic districts of western Switzerland, occupying the areas of the Vaud, the Chablais and the lower Valais, and establishing there the religion of "their Lordships of Berne". From then until the French revolution and even later, the Confederation was continually racked by wars, conflicts and intrigues between its Catholic and its reformed member-states.

A lot could be said of the primitive accumulation of capital in the pre-revolutionary Confederation. For instance: after the revocation of the Edict of Nantes, the role of the protestant bank of Geneva in handling capital illegally exported from France was extremely important.[4] In Zürich, the new ruling class took up the silk and cotton trade. In Berne, the first state treasury of the Confederation was set up. In the eighteenth century, Swiss farms numbered 740,000 head of cattle – a higher proportion of animal to human population than in 1970. From the eighteenth century on, 30,000 quintals of Gruyère cheese were exported into France every year. Horses were raised intensively, and several of Europe's armies bought exclusively from Swiss breeders. In short, though we have not got precise figures for all sectors, it is quite clear that the ruling classes of pre-industrial Switzerland went in for primitive capital accumulation in a big way.[5]

The revolution in Paris had the effect of revealing the contradictions existing in the Confederation: as Lucerne peasant mercenaries died fighting for the French king at the Tuileries, the banker Necker arranged for French aristocrats to get their money out to Geneva and London. The arrival of Napoleon marked the end of the *ancien régime*. The patricians returned to power for the last time after the French occupying troops left in 1814, but their day was over, and the comprador and industrial bourgeoisie – filled with long-suppressed democratic and egalitarian ideas – took control of one canton after another. There was a final ideological war (semi-religious, semi-political) in 1847: the member-states of the Confederation, under secular and centralist governments, fought the Catholic cantons whose governments were conservative and federalist. Reaction was defeated, and in 1848 the Confederal State was proclaimed.

Historically speaking, the present Radical electoral bureaucracy is the vehicle of that new urban bourgeoisie; the Liberal Party that of the displaced patricians; while the Christian Democrats are the party of the Catholic peasants and bourgeoisie. But it must be stressed that none of these parties today represents a social movement: they are electoral machines dealing in political favours and skilfully manipulating the real social conflicts that exist. They no longer bear any relation to reality – save in reflecting the decline of a political system that was admirable when it started.

The workers' movement, and the socialist and labour parties that are its political expression, are very different now from what they were at first. The new urban bourgeoisie of capitalists and traders who – thanks to a growing industry and the rapid development of a tertiary sector in the towns – had achieved power in sixteen out of twenty-two states by the middle of the nineteenth century (and exercised almost exclusive dominance over all federal bodies until 1874) found themselves under attack from 1840 on from a powerful workers' movement. Here are a few figures:[6] when the new ruling class gained political power, the industrial proletariat were still few in number, but they had a lively class consciousness, and their sector of the economy was an important one. In 1850, only 4 per cent of the active population worked in factories. But the industrial proletariat – the class in which the workers' movement is objectively rooted, and whence it derives its subjective class-consciousness – extended far beyond the factories. The main industries of the period, textiles and watchmaking, which accounted for about 80 per cent of all exports, functioned by way of a mixed system of factory work and home work. In 1850 there were over 350,000 men, women and children – i.e. 32.5 per cent of the active population – working for industry, in the most appalling working conditions and for the most appalling wages, at home, in workshops, in yards, on building sites, some full-time, some "seasonal". Furthermore, this industrial proletariat was concentrated in particular regions: the textile industry between Lake Constance and the Lake of Zürich, watchmaking in Geneva and the Jura. Both these sectors expanded rapidly after 1850. Between 1843 and 1856, the number of spindles for cotton-spinning rose from 660,000 to 1.15 million, an increase of 74 per cent. We find the beginnings of capital concentration and the first indications of monopolization. Despite the rapid growth of production, the number of enterprises remained virtually stable: 131 in 1843, 136 in 1856. But it was watchmaking that was to change the social history of the Swiss proletariat. In 1839, a worker called Georges Leschot invented a number of ingenious machine-tools. Two Genevan capitalists, Vacheron and Constantin, decided to exploit his skill: his machines made it possible to produce inter-changeable parts rapidly and in quantity. Homeworking disappeared; from now on, the proletariat of watchmaking flooded into the workshops.

We can list briefly the stages in the organization of the workers' movement:

First stage: 1864, the founding of the International. 1866, its first Congress in Geneva. Karl Marx clashes with Bakunin, and the Jurassian federations support the anarchist view.

Second stage: 1868, the first large strike in Switzerland takes place in Geneva.

Third stage: 1870, the founding of the Socialist Union in Zürich.

Fourth stage: 1888, the founding of the Swiss Socialist Party.

Fifth stage: 1918, general strike suppressed by the army.

Sixth stage: 1919, split in the Socialist Party, and birth of the Communist Party.

Seventh stage: 1937, the steelworkers' unions sign a truce with the employers for an indefinite period, whereby all strikes are to be submitted to arbitration beforehand. This agreement, known as the "Industrial Peace" agreement, remains in force today. It marked the beginning of the temporary decline of the workers' movement in Switzerland, and its present phase of partial collaboration with the national bourgeoisie and the imperialist oligarchy.

Let us now take a look at the institutions and mechanisms of the "visible" government:

The Federal Assembly,[7] the keystone of the system, consists of two chambers of equal political importance – for no law, no ordinary federal decree, no urgent federal decree can be enforced without having been debated in them both. All members of both have the same rights, above all the right to put forward legislative bills themselves, and get them passed by means (in order of decreasing importance) of an "individual initiative", a "motion", a "postulate", an "interjection" or a "challenge". Each chamber has its own powerful permanent committees (on finance, foreign affairs, military affairs, scientific research and foreign trade).

The first chamber is the National Council. Since 1919 it has been elected by proportional representation, with each member-state forming one electoral district. The National Council has two hundred members, fourteen of them women.[8] It is elected every four years, and at every election about one third of the councillors are replaced (usually for reasons of age – electoral defeat is relatively rare in Switzerland). The second chamber, the Council of States, is elected on a quite different basis. It has forty-four members (only one a woman), two for every member-state, with the half-cantons having one councillor each; the election is regulated by the laws of each canton. In Berne, for instance, the cantonal parliament chooses the two councillors, whereas in Geneva they are popularly elected. The National Council and the Council of States together constitute the Federal Assembly. It is an assembly that can only be said to be representative of the Swiss population in a very loose sense. The majority of the electors are aged between twenty and forty, but only seven per cent of councillors are in this age-group. Women represent 53 per cent of the electorate, yet only fifteen women are councillors at present. The national average income is around 18,000 francs a year, whereas the average declared income of the councillors is 53,000 francs. There are 1,350,000 manual workers in Switzerland, 366,000 of them women: there is only one manual worker in the assembly, and he is a man.

The Federal Assembly is an almost perfect reflection of the political class that has come into being over the centuries, whose immobility appears to be the outstanding feature of Swiss political life.[9]

Let us turn next to the election of the government: Switzerland lives under an assembly system that is, sociologically, quite similar to that of the Third Republic in France. The sovereign assembly – i.e. the two chambers meeting together – elects a government of seven members at the start of every legislature, for the four years of that legislature (in the early days of the Confederation it was a three-year period). In 1975, the Confederal State inaugurated its fortieth legislature. The way the government is elected is quite special: each of the seven posts is voted for separately – yet there is normally only one candidate for each! We in Switzerland dislike elections in which the outcome is unpredictable. We also dislike strong leaders: the seven federal councillors take it in turn to fill the posts of president and vice-president. No one can be president of the Confederation for more than twelve months running. With very few exceptions, federal councillors come from the assembly or the cantonal governments. Thus their wholehearted membership of the political class is guaranteed: they have usually had a long training in its way of life, and bring with them to the Federal Council the many friendships and occasional enmities, the sympathies, aversions and prejudices accumulated during lengthy service in their cantonal legislature or executive. To become a federal councillor is the dream of most parliamentarians, and the lucky ones who achieve it have generally spent decades (though sometimes only a few years) in that curious federal palace which faces one of the most beautiful landscapes in the world yet has absolutely no windows opening on to it. (This is no mere symbol: this imposing turn-of-the-century building has been fitted with a ludicrous and expensive system of artificial ventilation. Air from outside no longer enters it at all.) In short, once elected, the new federal councillor remains closely involved not only with his own party – even after their election federal councillors continue, like any other deputies and with the same rights, to attend regularly the meetings of their respective party groups in parliament – but with the whole rather neurotic world that exists behind the closed doors of the parliament. It is obvious that new ideas very rarely break into it.

As compared with a system like the French Third Republic, the visible government system of the Confederation presents at least two major deviations:

(1) The executive is not responsible to the legislature. (The exercise of power is collegial; but each of the seven federal councillors runs one of the seven executive departments of the Confederation. So it is within his particular department that the real power of the federal councillor makes itself felt.) The government cannot be turned out in the lifetime of an Assembly. In any case, even if there were such a thing as a vote of censure or a vote of confidence there would be little risk: of the 244 deputies to the Federal Assembly, only 41 belong to parties without any seats on the executive – and of those 23 are quite happy with the existing coalition. These are in the main deputies of the fascist-orientated right wing: Republicans and National Action, plus deputies who belong to the Alliance of independents, and a few liberals.

(2) The people have powerful rights. 100,000 citizens can call for an article in the constitution (or even the entire constitution) to be changed by means of an "initiative". If the initiative is accepted by the majority of the population and of the member-states, then the constitution is changed. In addition to this, any law passed in the Assembly can be contested by the citizens; it only needs 60,000 signatures to call for a referendum. But these popular rights have no real political significance unless they are exercised by free and well-informed citizens – citizens who are protected from the effects

of the oligarchy's symbolic violence. Of whom there are very few. Most of the time, our famous "direct democracy" is quitely transmuted into a direct oligarchy. Propaganda campaigns into which the oligarchy pour millions of francs usually overcome any resistance there may be from the populace or the trade unions. In most of the recent plebiscites, the people, obedient and dutiful as they are, have freely rejected any reform intended to increase their power, their well-being or their freedom. Consider, for instance: in 1962 and 1963 the people obediently rejected a ban on the production and stockpiling of atomic weapons on Swiss territory; in 1967, they turned down a law to stop property speculation; in 1970, they turned down a constitutional initiative on the right to housing; in 1973 they turned down the right to training; in 1974, still brainwashed, they refused obligatory federal sickness insurance, as well as old-age insurance – thus *freely* renouncing the introduction of social security in Switzerland! In 1976, a law on land use, intended to safeguard green space, was rejected. And on 21 March of that year came the crowning point: the overwhelming majority of Swiss workers turned down a constitutional initiative proposed by their own trade unions to introduce a measure of worker-participation into the management of their own firms.

How does one become a federal councillor? By persistently saying nothing, for a long time. At the very least, by intervening in public debate only with the greatest caution and the utmost vagueness. Only when one knows beforehand that unanimity is assured. For the system is one of co-option. But who co-opts whom? It is hard to say for sure. The Federal Assembly is controlled by shifting majorities. From time to time, the oligarchy will suddenly insist on putting in a man who is directly dependent on them. Certainly, both those federal councillors co-opted by parliament and those brought in as a result of press campaigns stage-managed by the oligarchy tend to be excellent administrators.

The Parliament, a theoretically admirable institution which symbolizes one phase in the history of the class struggle in Europe, naturally shares in the secondary characteristics of the state. This being said, however, we have to distinguish three levels of reality.

In matters of structural policy – when debating such major issues as the status of foreign banks in Switzerland, the role of the national bank, arms spending, etc. – Parliament's margin for manoeuvre is virtually nil. The secondary imperialist oligarchy make their own law.

When the deputies' debates (or the activities of government, administration, the press, etc.) do not directly affect the structure of the exploitative society, the way the oligarchy exercise their power, or the explanations they choose to give of it, then the Assembly has a very wide area of freedom. When it acts within that area, it often achieves wonders. For example: the new law worked out between 1971 and 1973 on adoption and citizenship, which resulted in one of the most progressive and humane solutions found anywhere in Europe to the problem of abandoned children.

There is also a third sphere in which the visible government can act – that of arbitration when two factions of the oligarchy have temporarily fallen out. For it can happen that two groups find themselves on opposing sides in a matter of real importance. The visible government then suddenly realizes that it has an unexpected taste of freedom. For example: the revaluation of the Swiss franc. The banking barons fought strenuously to prevent this, because their speculations in European and American currency required the franc to remain level. The companies dealing with imports and domestic distribution, however, wanted revaluation (the Migros distribution company were demanding a readjustment of as much as 12 per cent) so as to increase their profit margins. In this situation of conflict, the Federal Council was able to issue a surprise decree revaluing the Swiss franc by 7 per cent on 10 May 1971. By a recent change in federal law, only the government can determine the exchange rate.

Let us now look at the way the visible government, and more particularly the parliament, is colonized by the secondary imperialist oligarchy.

Like the kings of France, the imperialist oligarchy have a virtually inexhaustible supply of patronage possibilities at their disposal. The system is ingenious. The oligarchy control a huge number of property, finance, industrial and commercial companies; most of these are established as limited companies (*sociétés anonymes*). The colonization of the parliament is carried out as follows: as soon as a deputy from a bourgeois party is elected, the oligarchy evaluate his potential political weight, and offer him a seat on a management board or perhaps the chairmanship of an employers' association. Both jobs carry large salaries. During the 39th legislature, 82 per cent of all the members of the Federal Assembly belonged to one or more management boards.[10] There are 244 deputies in the two chambers, and among them they fill a total of over 1,000 directors' jobs. Of these, we should deduct about 250, which belong to publicly-owned companies (railways, power stations, and such), but that still leaves 750 jobs shared out among 115 deputies from the bourgeois parties. They include highly paid posts on the management boards of the banking empires, property companies, armaments industries, multinational industrial and commercial companies, both Swiss and foreign. Any deputy, whatever his social background, his professional experience or his personal capabilities, can become a millionaire the moment he is elected – provided he was elected on a bourgeois ticket and evinces enough docility combined with discretion and efficiency. But, even among these 115 deputies representing capital, there is a still smaller aristocracy who enjoy most of the oligarchy's favours: 81 bourgeois deputies from the two chambers fill among them 431 directors' jobs. For instance: one man, States Councillor Peter Hefti, from Glarus, holds 37 directorships in banks, multinational companies and property trusts. His colleague from Zürich, Fritz Honegger, holds 22, including one with Honeywell, the largest manufacturer of "anti-personnel" bombs in the world. The Catholic deputy, Paul Eisenring, from Zürich, holds 25 directorships, and the share-capital of his companies adds up to over 750 million francs.

These 115 representatives of the people, who once elected, are transformed into representatives of capital, now represent – at the lowest estimate – some 15 billion Swiss francs. This modest sum corresponds to a third of all the social capital of all the limited companies registered in Switzerland. But ours is a land of justice: even these sinecures are equitably shared out among the different bourgeois parties. 39 Radical Party deputies in parliament "represent" 284 banks, multinationals and property companies; the total social capital of their benefactors amounts to 6,830 million Swiss francs. As for the pious Christian democrats, they "represent" 334 banks, industrial trusts and armaments plants. 40 of them alone "represent" a company capital of 2,807 million Swiss francs.

This system sometimes leads to ludicrous situations. For example: a parliamentary debate in 1972. The pacifist deputy Arthur Villard denounced the use of the Swiss Pilatus-Porter plane in Vietnam by the American air force. This small and highly mobile plane can fly at tree-top level and is particularly useful for spotting small guerrilla units or villages lost in the forest: once people have been sighted, the pilot drops a smoke bomb to signal the target to the Phantom bombers, which arrive within minutes to burn the villagers to death. Villard demanded that the government ban the sale of Pilatus-Porters to the United States and their allies (particularly the Australians). But a deputy from Buochs came forward to declare that the Pilatus-Porter was a very slow and light plane unsuitable for carrying bombs or rockets, and that it could hardly be described as a war plane! The government and most of the deputies accepted this idea enthusiastically. The successful speaker, the deputy from Nidwald, was a man called August Albrecht: he was also chairman of the company that made the Pilatus-Porter, a subsidiary of the Bürhle-Oerlikon trust.

Another example: in 1974, there was a debate in parliament on the trade-union initiative seeking to get workers' participation in managing their firms. During my intervention, I quoted the magnificent example of successful self-management given by the Lip workers. There was a storm of protest. A deputy named Yann Richter rose to speak: in a fine flurry of eloquence he attacked me and declared that, objectively, the Lip workers were simply thieves. Wild applause! It may be noted that Richter is assistant director of the Swiss watch industry association; one member of that association is ASUAG, whose subsidiary, Ebauches SA, was a major shareholder in Lip in 1973.

To grasp the full extent and complexity of the oligarchy's control over the federal parliament and its related institutions (commissions of experts and so on), one must examine their various different strategies. First: they directly employ a certain number of loyal men, such as Paul Eisenring, an economist and editor of the *Handelszeitung,* or Fritz Honnegger, chairman of the Zürich Chamber of Commerce. They naturally do all they can to help these men to get into politics. It seems equally natural that, once elected, such people should join a considerable number of boards of directors of powerful financial groups. There is another, more common, path to promotion: men – and very occasionally, women – get into parliament from social positions or professions in which they had never attracted notice from the oligarchy. However, the moment they are elected, similar offers are made to them.[11]

For example: A Radical deputy from Geneva, Fernand Corbat, who had worked in an advertising firm, became president of the Swiss cigarette manufacturers' association the day after his election. A woman who had taught French in her local university was elected to the Council of States, and at once joined the management board of one of the three national banking empires. The list is too long to give here. But we may add that most local jurists, councillors and lawyers, however little they know about finance, become important company lawyers as soon as they are elected on a bourgeois ticket. Many instances could be cited: from Baden, a small town near Zürich, to Lugano – not excluding the tiny town of Schwyz.

With the Federal Council, it is the same story. In theory being a member of the government is incompatible with holding any other paid job; none the less, there is a steady circulation of people between the management boards of the financial and industrial empires and the government. The channels were established during the great venture of building the Alpine railways – which demanded the closest collaboration between the federal executive and the banks that invested such colossal sums in the work. Here is how the oligarchy "use" the Federal Council:

Some of those elected are already in the employ of hegemonic big business, even before they are elected. When their term of office is over, they return to their former sphere but with appropriate promotion. For example: Max Petitpierre, a company lawyer in Neuchâtel, was president of the Swiss watchmakers' association before joining the government as Minister of Foreign Affairs. When he left, he rose to the chairmanship of the management board of Nestlé. Hans Schaffner, a leading federal civil servant specialising in matters of international trade, became Minister of the Economy. On leaving the ministry, he quite naturally became vice-president of the Sandoz empire (chemicals, and pharmaceutical products). Nello Celio, a company lawyer in Lugano, president of the multinational trust Alusuisse (aluminium and bauxite) was the intelligent and sophisticated ideologist of forward-thinking top management. He was of course promoted to the Federal Council, and there, again of course, became Minister of Finance. His term ended in 1974, and he is now the key man on a large number of the major banking and industrial boards where the oligarchy's strategy is worked out.

As far as one can see, none of these men ever abused his powers when in government in order to benefit any of the trusts of which he is now director. It is more a matter of a "natural reflex" on the part of the Swiss system: such promotions merely illustrate the profound logic inherent in it, the ontological harmony between the interests of the state and the strategy of accumulating private capital.

The second form of promotion occurs when men who have risen from the petty or middle bourgeoisie, or very occasionally from farming, and have no previous connexion with the oligarchy, are co-opted to the Federal Council. On leaving, they are promoted to be members of the management boards of multinational companies. Here too, examples are endless, and I will give only one: Paul Chaudet, a vine-grower from Rivaz, on the shore of Lake Léman, became a state councillor in the Vaud, then a national councillor, and finally Minister of the Armed Forces. Today he is president of the Banque Populaire Suisse, one of the most powerful banking empires in Europe. Nello Celio declared to Roger Dubois: "I promise you that there has never been a federal councillor who did favours to industry to get a place on a board of directors. Not one."[12]

Perhaps not. But no one has any way of checking up on what a deputy or a minister does. Given that the 1848 Federal Constitution expressly denies that deputies are bound to represent the views of their constituents, they can always claim that their votes and decisions are a matter of free choice, each one voting purely as his clear conscience dictates. Members of the Swiss government generally remain in office for many years. Here is an instance of the sort of thing I find shocking: Max Petitpierre was Foreign Minister for twenty-two years; but the moment he left the government, he joined Nestlé as chairman of the board of directors. By that time, all the existing ambassadors and most of the senior staff of the ministry owed their jobs to him. Clearly this network of diplomatic relations, with so many people dependent on Petitpierre and under his thumb, must be invaluable to a multinational company producing 98 per cent of its goods abroad – the world's largest manufacturer of babyfoods and powdered milk.

Let us look next at two other structures parallel to this colonized parliament: the hierarchy of the armed forces, and the hierarchy of the parliamentary "lobbies".

Switzerland has a militia of some 620,000 men.[13] Apart from the senior officers and a small body of instructors – officers and NCOs – everyone is obliged to do military service on a temporary, national service basis. All field officers – other than colonels commanding a division or an army corps (there are no generals in peacetime) – are unpaid militiamen.

The role of the army in Switzerland is not easily analysed; however, it has four immediately recognizable functions:

1. It genuinely serves to ensure the defence of Swiss territory against the ever-present possibility of foreign aggression.

2. It preserves (monopolist and capitalist) order inside the country.

3. It is the instrument for the process of integrating the different nationalities of which the Confederation is composed.

4. It is necessary for the maintenance of the military-industrial complex, and the profits that complex makes for the oligarchy.

Most deputies-cum-businessmen also hold positions of command in the army. If you want to be a federal councillor it is very useful to have been a colonel in the militia. Once an officer becomes a member of the National Council or the Council of States, only death can prevent his rising to the rank of colonel. His "bosses" – the leaders of the secondary imperialist oligarchy – are often in the army themselves, as staff- or field-officers. (The whole system has its paradoxical aspects. Militia officers, given their often highly privileged social situation in civilian life, make considerable sacrifices of time and money to serve in the army. This seems to them to justify whatever advantages they may gain in civilian life as a result of their rank in the army, while at the same time it virtually bars anyone from the working class from reaching the higher ranks.) This situation is unique in Europe. To take a couple of examples: the present commander-in-chief of the army, Colonel-Corps Commander Vischer, belongs to one of the reigning families in the Basle chemical industry; and Dieter Bührle, the managing director of one of the most powerful armaments companies in Europe, is a colonel of the militia.

As always, the army is social violence institutionalized. As experience has shown, it serves both to defend national sovereignty against foreign enemies and to combat "the enemy within". In Switzerland, the enemy within consists of any group, party, movement, trade union or organization that threatens the political hegemony of the imperialist oligarchy. Maintaining public order also means maintaining the order of monopoly capitalism (for example, military repression of the general strike of 1918, of the workers' demonstration in Geneva in 1932, and so on). Thus it fits in with the fundamental logic of the system that most of our military leadership consists of leading figures from the world of finance capital and members of parliament. It is not the militia system that I am again criticizing here, much less the existence of the army as a means of national defence; it is only the class bias of its hierarchy, its interests, its decisions and therefore its politics.

There is, as I have said, a second parallel structure: some members of the Federal Assembly, even though they may belong to different parties, are linked to the same financial interests; these people form what may be called lobbies within the Assembly, known harmlessly enough as "parliamentary groups". Some such pressure groups wield enormous power, either by way of the parliamentary committees they control, or by the direct pressure they can bring to bear on both the government and public opinion.[14]

Here are some examples: there is a group for commerce and

industry, a group for traffic, tourism and the hotel industry, a group for planning and land use, a parliamentary press group, a group for internal navigation, the political and social group for the radical members, and so on.[15]

A study of the interwoven structures controlling the Federal Assembly – the keystone of the official power system in Switzerland – leads one to the question of precisely how they interact, and especially of just how much direct influence the secondary imperialist oligarchy have on parliamentary decision-making. There can certainly be no straightforward mechanistic answer. Surely all these parliamentarians – many of them extremely highly-paid –[16] must be tempted to let their voting be influenced by self-interest when they have to deal with a law that touches the affairs of their banks, multinational companies, armanents works or real estate trusts. Of course, they swear by all that is sacred that they can keep the two things separate, that they can as deputies vote in favour of a law which as individuals they deplore. One thing seems certain: when the people elect their deputies, they do not expect them at once to start working, even only part of the time, for real estate companies or merchant banks. Yet, significantly enough, the problem is never discussed in public, except by the trade unions or the parties of the Left. On the one hand, these people are re-elected over and over again, and most of our newspapers never refer to the problem; on the other, they themselves present a front that even the most intelligent political commentators never formally challenge. In 1973, Julius Binder, a conservative deputy from Baden, led the way to actually reinforcing the "smokescreen". He put forward a motion demanding increased administrative powers for the Assembly so as to preserve this parliament of "volunteers" and prevent the establishment of a "professional" parliament. The argument ran as follows: a "parliament of volunteers", consisting of deputies who earn their living in ordinary jobs, and therefore remain close to their fellow-citizens, is more "representative" than a parliament composed of professional deputies, whose only occupation is to represent the people. At first sight, this is an attractive theory,[17] but its further implications are pretty evident: the Swiss Assembly, the only European parliament whose members receive no salary, demands considerable financial sacrifices from them. To make up for this, it is therefore quite "natural" and "right" that the deputies, once they are elected, should yield to the urgings of the real estate companies, banks and multinational corporations, and join their boards of directors. The rich life style – the gift of the oligarchy – then appears to be a kind of reward offered to these virtuous servants of the people who have momentarily sacrificed prospects of personal gain in order to work for the common weal. Thus the colonization of the Assembly becomes miraculously invested with the dignity of an ontological necessity.

Notes to Chapter 6

1. As a result of the campaign of the Jurassians for liberation and independence, a twenty-third member-state is soon to come into being. It consists in the main of old French-speaking districts in the north occupied by the state of Berne in 1815. The new state of Jura is expected to be voted into the confederation in 1978.

2. A.Touraine, *La Production de la société,* Paris (Seuil), 1973, pp.34ff.

3. The mutiny of the Lullin regiment left one odd legacy: a party of soldiers condemned to the galleys were marched through the streets of Paris with iron collars on. They were liberated by the mob. During the spontaneous celebrations, some of the Parisians put on the caps worn by the galley-convicts: these caps, known as "Phrygian caps", were later to become the liberty caps that symbolized the Republic. Cf. W.Martin, *Histoire de la Suisse,* Lausanne (Payot).

4. H.Luthy, *La Banque protestante en France, op. cit.,* especially vol. II, *Dispersion et Regroupement 1685-1730.*

5. W.Martin, *op. cit.*

6. Figures for the beginnings of Swiss industry are from J.F.Bergier, *Naissance et Croissance de la Suisse industrielle,* Berne (Franks), 1974.

7. Deputies receive no salary, but they get expenses of 150 francs every day parliament sits, and a lump sum of 10,000 francs a year.

8. These are the figures for the 1971-75 legislature.

9. A certain positivist school of sociology (cf. E.Gruner *et al., L'Assemblée fédérale, 1848-1920,* vol. II, Berne, 1972) has shown how a kind of hereditary institutional power is handed down in families in some cantons. It is quite true that there are endless sons and cousins and brothers of political figures of the past in parliament today. It is also true that virtual political aristocracies have come to exist in some cantons, especially in the Alps. One can, for instance, visit the cemetery in Altdorf, capital of the canton of Uri, where all the deceased members of the leading families are buried under a monument listing their titles and functions. However, it is not the development of dynastic aristocracies that constitutes the real problem of the colonization of parliament.

10. For a list of names, cf. the *Annuaire des conseils d'administration,* Zürich (Annonces-Mossé).

11. Unlike the United States, France or Britain, the Swiss Parliament expressly refuses to enquire into such matters. On 18 June 1975, one deputy asked that an official list of deputies with company-directorships be set up. His proposal was turned down. The bureau of the National Council replied that "There is no legal basis for such a list". And that was that. (Cf. doc. CN no. 75.738.)

12. When the first edition of this book appeared, the oligarchy mustered all their journalists to discredit the book and its author, its politics and its information. The supposedly neutral national press directed a barrage of cleverly written abuse at the book to alienate readers. Television tried to censor comments, and the French-speaking Swiss radio banned all discussion of the book. Roger Dubois had the courage, intelligence and honesty to confront members of the oligarchy and their agents with the facts presented in the book, and he published their replies in a series of six articles in the *Tribune de Genève* in May 1976. Roger Dubois died on 9 August 1976: I here pay him the heartfelt homage of my esteem and gratitude.

13. The best work on the Swiss army is in English: *The Defence Forces of Switzerland,* one of a series of books on "Armies of the World". It is published by *The Army Quarterly and Defence Journal* (West of England Press), 1974.

14. D.Sidjanski, "Les groupes de pression et la politique étrangère en Suisse", *Annuaire de l'Association suisse de science politique,* 1966.
15. The list can be found in G.Keel-Nguyen, "L'influence des groupes d'intérêts politiques sur la politique étrangère de la Suisse", in *Handbuch der Aussenpolitik,* Berne (Haupt), 1975.
16. The multinational companies and banking businesses pay their director-deputies attendance money amounting to anything between 80,000 and 220,000 Swiss francs a year on average. It is not uncommon to find an especially influential deputy with a seat on several dozen boards. The record was held by a deputy in the 38th legislature, who held 61 directorships.
17. And many writers see nothing wrong with it : see Erich Gruner *et al., Assemblée fédérale et peuple suisse, 1848-1920*; Leonhard Neidhart, "Die Funktion des parlementarisch-repräsentativen Elementes", in *Die Reform des Bundesstaates,* 1970.

Appendix to Part II

(A book of this kind cannot overlook the xenophobia of a proportion of the Swiss people, nor the policy of apartheid practised by the ruling class and their government. The immigrant worker suffers from economic, political, social and ideological repression. The important study by Delia Castelnuovo-Frigessi, "Colonialismo a domicilio: i lavoratori stranieri in Svizzera", could well have figured as an appendix to any one of the preceding chapters. However, I have a particular reason for quoting from it here at the end of the section on symbolic violence – the author, through her analysis of Swiss apartheid legislation, shows how the image of the immigrant labourer, the "foreigner" – without a home, without a family, without any rights – is used by the imperialist oligarchy. The exploitation of the immigrant labourer, the "foreigner", is a function of the structural violence of imperialism.[1] It has identifiable material causes. But it is made possible – i.e. generally acceptable – because of the image of the "foreigner", the man who is "different", that the oligarchy has managed to foist on to the Swiss working class.

The legislation, the statistics, the international agreements governing the underprivileged lives of foreign workers in Switzerland are changing all the time. Things will be different in one respect or another by the time this book is published. However, Delia Castelnuovo-Frigessi's study still unmasks the nature of the institutional strategy used by the oligarchy to exploit the immigrant labourer.)

Colonialism at home: Immigrant workers in Switzerland

Having for centuries been a land of emigrants, Switzerland has become in our day a land of immigrants. Between 1850 and 1888, emigration continued higher than immigration (a difference of 177,000), but between 1888 and 1914, the opposite became the case (the difference being 176,000). The maximum figure for immigration reached in 1914 (around 600,000, or 15.4 per cent of the total population) was approached again in 1960 (584,739); in 1968, foreigners represented 15.3 per cent of the total population, as they did in 1914, and the percentage has continued to rise in the intervening years. The Federal Police estimates for 1972 give the following statistics: "At the end of December, the Swiss economy gave work in all – including *frontaliers* [workers living just over the border], seasonal workers, those with yearly work permits and those in permanent residence – to 708,815 foreign workers. . . . This figure represents 23 per cent of the active population of Switzerland, bringing the total up to about 3,075,000. If one takes the peak figures recorded in August, the proportion of foreign workers is as high as 27 per cent of the working population."

The country's immigration policy has passed through several different phases. The first was from 1917 to 1925 (free movement from one country to another having been stopped from the time of the First World War). It was during these years that the first laws for police supervision of foreigners were passed (21 February 1917; 19 November 1921). Permits began to be required for visiting the country, and for working and living there. Under certain conditions, people were banned from entering the country (art. 10 of the Regulation for the Control of Foreign Immigration, 29 November 1921); a system of consultation was set up (art. 17) between the cantonal police and the cantonal labour offices; new distinctions were introduced establishing different categories of residence for foreigners (for limited or indefinite periods), and we find the first reference to seasonal workers. In the communiqué from the Federal Council to the Federal Assembly on regulations for foreign visitors and residents (2 June 1924) it was all brought for the first time within the officially-declared framework of a *selective* immigration policy. In 1924, for the first time, foreigners were classified "according to new criteria relating specifically to preventing the growth of too large a foreign population; foreign visitors have little effect on that population, since by definition they depart again, but foreigners who make their homes here must be taken fully into account". The principle of guarding against an over-large foreign population – with its suggestion of war-time vocabulary – gradually became widely established. Xenophobia was in fact brought into being and fuelled by the ruling class.

Still quoting from the same Federal Council message, preventing the foreign population from becoming too large meant "the adoption of a new criterion for admission, that is, the country's capacity to receive them". To regulate the influx of this labour force to suit the demands of the economy, it was proposed to institute new legislation. The effective instrument of that legislation was to be a police force to deal specifically with foreigners, whose official task was to ensure jobs for the Swiss by protecting them against competition from foreign labour.

Over the years since a quota has been in force, the numbers of seasonal workers (but not of other categories) have been restricted according to the type of work done: in 1965 and 1966, building workers were limited to 145,000 and 125,000 respectively; in 1967, 115,000 foreigners were allowed in for building work, 21,000 for hotel work, and 16,000 for various industrial jobs. In the 1970 decree these numbers remained the same. Up until 1973, the federal government continued to take the line that seasonal workers and *frontaliers* "do not have the same effect as non-seasonal workers in terms

119

of invasion of foreigners".

After 1954, the proportions of the different types of workers allowed in by permit (not including those already settled here) changed, as is clear from the figures given in the review, *Vie économique,* for the years 1956-1973.

The number of workers with annual permits showed a rising curve from 1956 to 1969 (the sharpest rise being in 1964), and then gradually went down from 1970 to 1973. The number of seasonal workers, on the other hand, rose from 1956 to 1964, gradually went down till 1969, rose again in 1970 and reached a peak of 196,632 in 1972 (this was the total in August, but the number of visitors' permits issued in 1972 was actually 244,603). In 1972, seasonal workers went up by 8.7 per cent. In 1973, because of the measures adopted by the Federal Council, there were 2,866 fewer. *Frontaliers* have increased steadily since 1956: in 1972 the total had gone up by 10.7 per cent, in 1973 by 7.6 per cent.

In 1956, seasonal workers and *frontaliers* represented almost half of those subject to control (181,000 on yearly permits, 108,000 seasonal and 37,000 *frontaliers*). In 1964, there were 465,000 on yearly permits, 206,000 seasonal workers, and 49,000 *frontaliers*. The proportion of seasonal workers and *frontaliers* has gradually risen. Between 1970 and 1973, workers on yearly permits went down by 120,254, while seasonal workers and *frontaliers* went up by 82,797 (44,565 and 38,232 respectively). The latter group thus tends to make up for the reduction in the former. The increase in foreign residents, following the heavy immigration of the sixties, is seen as a necessary evil; they have to have worked ten years in the country before getting a permanent resident's permit. If we add together the residents and those with annual permits – who both enjoy certain privileges denied to other, "lower" categories of foreign workers – the figures appear as follows:

276,568 permanent residents	193,766 seasonal workers (August 1973)
322,513 on yearly permits	104,573 *frontaliers* (August 1973)
599,081	298,339

Thus, seasonal workers and *frontaliers* represent over a third of all the foreign workers in Switzerland. But when one adds the ever-rising number (reckoned to be between 25,000 and 30,000) of illegal workers who come to work for a few months in such places as Geneva, then our totals are some 600,000 foreign workers with a recognized legal status as compared with 330,000 or so temporary workers with no rights at all. This would suggest that now, more than ever, the composition of the foreign workforce is such as to favour economic exploitation based on political control and institutionalized discrimination. Substituting one category for another has made it possible to maintain the work-force demanded by the economy while increasing the proportion of workers with rights – who cost less and who, in times of economic crisis or stagnation, can be got rid of without any trouble. At the present time, as the greatest European recession since the war gets under way, this policy is clearly an indispensable weapon for the ruling oligarchy.

Seasonal workers may be described as the "strategic pillar" of the Swiss labour market. Their status is a solely negative one. They are allowed no mobility, either of place or of job. During the season they cannot change employers, yet they have no job security. They are not allowed – except in rare cases – to bring their families into Switzerland; a seasonal worker's wife extra to the quota may very occasionally be allowed to come and work (in a hospital, for instance), but never on any other basis. A recent regulation forbids any woman with children under age from coming at all, thus trying to end the abuse whereby some parents brought children in illegally and kept them with them. Such children (there are about 10,000 of them) cannot go to school or lead the normal life of children of their age, since they have to stay hidden indoors all day for fear of being found by the aliens' police, and deported. By law, the employer is bound to provide housing for the seasonal worker, but the lodging provided is seldom anything that could be described as a home – it is not always even furnished. Seasonal workers are packed like sardines, usually in the most insanitary conditions, in buildings far from any urban or social centre, or in old houses scheduled for demolition. "Housing" of this kind – on which the employer frequently makes an outrageous profit – isolates the seasonal worker; he lives more or less in a ghetto, on the fringes of society. Seasonal workers have to pay tax, but seldom make any use of the services provided by the state (schools, subsidized houses, etc.). Their tax is reckoned on the basis of a national wage higher than the wages they in fact receive, and multiplied by eleven months – yet, by the terms of their seasonal work contracts, they are forced to be out of work much of the time. Finally, they have to undergo health-checks when they enter the country, at the start of every season, and can be turned away because of an illness contracted *in* Switzerland during the previous season.

The ways in which seasonal workers are discriminated against speak volumes – a glaring instance of colonialism at home, whereby the foreign proletariat are condemned to political non-existence, legalized discrimination and social isolation. They are exploited by being allotted a precise role (in the most laborious and least well-paid jobs) in exchange for a precarious status and a job they could lose at any time. The ruling class derive certain specific advantages from their slave status. These include, among others: (1) A saving in public expenditure (including the cost of training the workers): the seasonal worker who cannot have his family with him makes proportionately less use – and then not full-time – of the public services (housing, hospitals, transport) schools, old people's homes, etc; (2) A flexible labour market: it is officially recognized that a seasonal workforce is far more manageable than a non-seasonal one – the workers can be dismissed virtually without notice.

> "The idea that seasonal workers do not constitute an addition to the foreign population is not wholly correct. They are also a burden on our services. It is primarily due to seasonal workers that the housing problem has become acute on several occasions, and has provoked lengthy public debate. The illegal presence in Switzerland of numbers of wives and children of foreign seasonal workers is frequently troublesome. Experience has shown that seasonal workers are the first to become involved in industrial disputes. Internationally, too, the problem of seasonal workers has caused Switzerland considerable difficulty."

This passage from the explanatory text that accompanied the new plan for regulating foreign migrant labour, distributed by the Federal Council on 28 May 1973, is a masterpiece of hypocrisy and cynicism. It sets out to make seasonal workers scapegoats in public opinion, to present them as a danger to the life of the Confederation both at home and abroad.

The new decree of July 1973 stipulated:

(1) A ceiling of 192,000. But when one recalls that the total in August of the preceding year was only 194,000, it is clear that the Federal Council was merely confirming an existing situation.

(2) The division of seasonal workers into quotas per canton (instead of per type of job), as with annual permit-holders; and their subdivision into two further categories: those lucky enough to have been working in the country in 1973 who could hope to

become annual permit-holders, and those doomed to remain seasonal workers forever (either new ones coming into the building trade or others whose contracts had been discontinued in 1972). The second were only authorized to stay in Switzerland for less than nine months, and had not, and never would have, any right to become annual permit-holders. Thus foreign workers were now classified in five categories instead of four. A similar change for the worse was made in the status of the *frontaliers,* another "safety valve" of the Swiss economy: they were not yet included in any quota system (120,000 in 1973) but they too were subjected to a new *apartheid*: anyone who wanted a work permit had to live regularly in the frontier zone for at least six months, and must go back every day.

The nine-month "season", the new basis of the seasonal worker's status, corresponds to nothing in real life. As long ago as 1957, if not earlier, the category of so-called "faux saisonniers" came into being. In that year, work on building sites which had always previously shut down on 30 November was continued until 15 December, with skilled workers expected to return on 1 March. Bit by bit, the building "season" was extended till it lasted for over eleven months. For the past ten years, seasonal workers have been able to work from early January. In 1970, the federal police gave employers permission to bring in half of their allotted seasonal workers on 4 January 1971, while the remainder could come in February. Thus the nine-month season no longer existed in the building trade. The Swiss government then came to an agreement with the Italian government to give yearly permits to those who qualified for them. But there was a delay in putting the agreement into effect, which had unfortunate effects on the family life of these workers because of the very long separations involved (57 per cent of the seasonal workers who came in 1973 were married men).

The contradiction between Swiss xenophobia and the economic and political forces governing the country is only apparent.[2] It is true that the xenophobic Right has found ready listeners among the sectors of the population who feel – and indeed, are – frustrated and exploited by big business, especially when they fulminate with convincing demagoguery against the damaging effects of capitalism on the working class. Though they are not genuinely anti-capitalist, they do disrupt the plans of the ruling class by demanding such a reduction in the foreign labour force as would have catastrophic effects on the national economy. Furthermore, they make abundantly clear the contradiction between the internationalism of the ruling bourgeoisie and the political isolationism of large sectors of the population. However, all this is merely secondary : objectively, this xeno-phobia serves the interest of the oligarchy, in that it drives an even deeper wedge between the Swiss workers and their foreign counter-parts.

Notes to Appendix to Part II

1. It really is, objectively, violence. Though there are some magistrates with scruples, and though a highly-placed young progressive civil servant, Jean-Pierre Bonny, has recently been appointed director of the Federal Bureau of industry, arts and trades with a special responsibility for migrant workers, these are only decorative extras which have little real political effect.

2. During this crisis period, there was an upsurge of right-wing xenophobic movements – the Republican Movement, led by James Schwarzenbach, and Action Nationale. Both groups condemned the Federal Council's policy towards immigrant labour as too permissive.

III
Pseudo-Neutrality

7
The "Theory" of Neutrality

"The Swiss, remaining neutral during the great revolutions in the states all around them, grew rich on the misfortunes of others, and founded a bank upon human disasters," said Chateaubriand Swiss neutrality[2] is a concept used with skill and persistence by the imperialist oligarchy to disguise what they are really doing: the mercenary state and its government are merely their echo. But one must beware of over-simplifying: that fictitious neutrality is historically linked with the rise of capitalism, but has not been totally determined by it. Swiss neutrality was ratified by the European powers at the Peace of Westphalia in 1648, and was renewed and confirmed by the powers at the Congress of Vienna in 1815. On the latter occasion, the Swiss diplomat Pictet-de-Rochemont won acceptance for the theory still loudly proclaimed by the Confederation today: Switzerland is neutral not for its own sake, but for the sake of others, for the presence of a neutral state in the heart of Europe is in the interest of every other state on the continent.

How, today, is this neutrality claimed by the visible government of the country formally defined? Even the merest statement of it is at once open to varying interpretations and disagreements. Etymologically, the word "neutral" comes from the Latin adjective *neuter,* or the medieval Latin *neutralis,* meaning "neither of the two". It is thus essentially a negative definition. If C is neutral, it is neither A nor B; or, to be more precise, the definition of A and B is totally independent of the definition of C, whereas the definition of C depends on the form and the semantic content of the definition of A and B. The neutral is first and foremost *neither of them.*[3] What is it, then?

André Gorz says, "Switzerland does not exist",[4] in the sense that a state which consistently withdraws from the international scene, which refuses to take sides and at times even denies the existence of the conflicts by which people and nations are racked, has no real international existence. As we have seen, this is not the case. Switzerland most certainly does exist. In fact it is a significant imperialist power. We must therefore move beyond the semantic debate to a more meaningful level of reality – the way in which the imperialist oligarchy and the visible government actually see themselves. Both are agreed on one point: neutrality is positive. What is it, then? Here is the definition given by a former Federal Councillor who afterwards became Chairman of Nestlé:

> Recent events, and the occasion they have given us to perform certain modest functions, seem to me to demonstrate that there is still room in the world today for a neutrality like that of our country; it is not a moral or a callous neutrality; it is not the same as neutralism; it is not running away from responsibility; it does not involve any dereliction of the duty to judge events; it does not shrink from action when action would serve the cause of peace.[5]

However, the positive side of neutrality rests also on another idea: it implies the notion of armed defence, of independence. Switzerland is neutral, it is not allied with any of the protagonists in a conflict. But should that conflict spill over into Swiss territory, should it threaten Swiss neutrality – i.e. Swiss independence – then Switzerland will take up arms to defend itself. Blankhart says rightly that "neutrality is a kind of local pacifism that reserves the right to defend itself".[6]

Finally, there is a third idea involved in our "neutrality" – the idea of mediation, Pictet-de-Rochemont told Metternich at Vienna that Swiss neutrality was in the interest of all the states of Europe. The role of mediator, claimed by the visible government, is in fact a fairly modest one. Essentially, it consists in the theoretical possibility of two enemies meeting on neutral ground. It is a geographical role rather than a political one. For example, in 1962, when the Swiss government offered the services of the ambassador, Olivier Long, to the two belligerents in the Algerian war, and he shuttled back and forth carrying messages between the Algerian Provisional Government delegation staying at Signal de Bougy, in Canton de Vaud, and the French negotiators staying in the Château de Leusse in the Haute Savoie, they were indeed offering a useful service. But in the event, the actual role played by the ambassador was that of postman rather than that of mediator. Since the Second World War, the Swiss government has never taken up – or rather has never had occasion to exercise – a genuine function of mediation. Real mediation would mean becoming a neutral third party in a conflict between two enemies, and being able, by the fact of that neutrality, to bring together opposing points of view, and gradually lead to their reconciliation – in other words, to end the conflict. The positive function of Swiss neutrality does not, in practice, include this sort of mediation at all.[7]

What, then, does Swiss neutrality mean in the day-to-day life of the country? Blankhart defines it clearly :

> Neutrality, like any foreign policy, is a policy for defending our interests. It has a specific positive aim – to preserve national sovereignty. But this does not alter the fact that neutrality in itself, whatever its aim, is purely negative. Furthermore, it must of necessity remain negative. Its negativeness can be accompanied by certain demonstrations of solidarity in the non-military sphere, but they must never be such as to render it any less negative. For anyone who wants to be neutral, there is only one kind of neutrality. No one can be a bit neutral. It would be a contradiction in terms.[8]

Swiss neutrality has therefore to be purely negative. Or, to paraphrase Claude Lévi-Strauss, it is an end in itself.

Notes to Chapter 7

1. The theory I am concerned with is the theory produced by the collective super-ego of the oligarchy themselves. It is here that those whom Gramsci might have called the indispensable "organic intelligentsia" of the secondary imperialist system come in.
2. There is an official text which defines our neutrality: cf. *Jurisprudence des autorités administratives de la Confédération,* year 1954, fascicule 24, p.9. The section is headed "Relations with other countries; the concept of neutrality".
3. For the etymology of the term, cf. F.Blankhart, "Der Neutralitätsbegriff aus logischer Sicht", *Mélanges Edgar Bonjour,* Helbling, Basle (Lichtenhan), 1968, pp.607ff.
4. A.Gorz, quoted in J.Halliday, "Switzerland, the Bourgeois Eldorado", *Quaderni Piacentini,* no. 39, November 1969, p.206.
5. M.Petitpierre, quoted in J.Freymond, "Neutralité et neutralisme", *Revue des travaux de l'Académie des sciences morales et politiques,* Paris, 1966, p.98.
6. Blankhart, *op.cit.,* p.617.
7. I.Galtung, in Büchi, Matter *et al., op. cit.,* p.vii.
8. Blankhart, *op. cit.*

8

The Colonization of Foreign Policy

The colonization of Swiss foreign policy is effected by a number of concurrent, or complementary means. First and most important is the control – or at least the infiltration – of the key institution of foreign policy, the Department of Trade,[1] by the banking oligarchy and the Vorort.[2]

Our Department of Trade is a curious and fascinating institution. It numbers 133 officials, the élite of the federal administration. In theory, it is subject to the federal Department of Public Economy; in practice, it does whatever it wants. The men who run it (a director, and four trade delegates with ambassadorial rank) are top-ranking technocrats: intelligent, quick-thinking, capable men, with friends on whom they can totally depend in every major government office in the world. As negotiators they are unequalled, but they are totally lacking in critical judgement when it comes to the politics of the imperialist oligarchy at home, or of the American government. The staff of the Department of Trade cultivate an Anglo-Saxon way of life, speak several languages, and work incredibly hard.

The Department of Trade controls the foreign trade of Switzerland. But it does a great deal more than that: it is a kind of vast analytical laboratory, where reasearch is done into the world economic situation, "advice" is given, and vital national decisions are planned – such as the agreement with the EEC, or Switzerland's joining the International Energy Agency. Consequently, in practice if not in theory, it is the Department of Trade that determines the country's foreign policy.

Given the degree of osmosis, the community of views, the interchange of personnel between the banking and industrial oligarchy and the Department, it is quite hard to discover which of the two controls the other. Or, to put it another way, though it is understood that the Department of Trade itself has no power, and that all economic and financial, and therefore all political, power is in the hands of the oligarchy, the complexity of hegemonic capital is such that it is impossible for outside observers – and probably even for the people concerned – to know who, in the decision-making process, actually uses, applies and directs that power.

For example: Is it the ambassador, Jollès[3] and the analyses he makes, or the managing director, de Weck[4] and the action he takes, that is responsible for the present tacit policy of support for the racist régime of South Africa by the Union Bank of Switzerland? Who organized the strangulation of Allende's Chile? Was it the Department of Trade, by cutting the federal export guarantee covering the plant and machinery asked for by the Allende government, or the industrialists who refused to deliver the spare parts and new machines? And, finally, who put the provision of oil to Switzerland into the hands of the aggressive cartel organized by Kissinger (the International Energy Agency), thus abandoning the independent line of bilateral agreements and objectively fostering an anti-Third World policy? Was this the result of the usual instrumental relationship of Swiss secondary imperialism to American imperialism, or of the analysis of the situation by the Department of Trade?

One cannot be sure. All one can say – and this is essential to any understanding of the practical steps by which the oligarchy achieve their colonization of foreign policy – is that there is an extraordinary closeness, an intellectual and psychological collusion between the directors of the Department and those of the multinational corporations of banking and industry.[5]

I remember a marvellous evening party in Basle in August 1973. The Foreign Trade Committee of the National Council were guests of the captains of the chemical industry, in the Hôtel des Trois Rois, a splendid building beside the Rhine, owned by the pharmaceutical trusts. The managing director of Ciba-Geigy, a tall, nervous, entertaining fellow, gave a talk to explain to us simple parliamentarians why our monetary policy (we had just decided to let the franc float) was totally inept. His tone was kind but firm. He was followed by another speaker, his financial director, Schaer. His speech was rather more aggressive in tone – the rising young executive showing his employers that he knew how to take a tough line with the enemy. Immediately in front of me sat a dignified old gentleman who kept nodding his approval: this was Staehlin, President of the Swiss Bank Corporation, who was responsible for the victory of Von Planta in the long war of intrigue which preceded the merging of Ciba and Geigy. At last it was time for the dinner they were giving us. Schaer announced that they had arranged the seating-plan so as to have either a representative of Ciba-Geigy, or someone from the Department of Trade, at every table. Their job would be to explain to us uneducated parliamentarians where Switzerland's real

interests lay, and what our monetary policy should be. I did not stay for the dinner.

This interpenetration between the Department of Trade and the secondary imperialist oligarchy is one of the political factors that determine Swiss foreign policy. For example: the multinational Hoffmann-La Roche company has one of the largest pharmaceutical laboratories in the world. In poor countries, its vitamins and tranquillizers are sold at very high prices. Complaints are heard that it operates a cartel pricing policy in Europe, where the rules of community competition were laid down in the 1972 Treaty between Switzerland and the EEC. Stanley Adams, one of the company's officers, laid a complaint about the cost of valium (with evidence to support it) before Albert Borschette, the European commissioner responsible for competitive trading, in Brussels – who had in fact already been keeping an eye for some months on the way the market for vitamins and tranquillizers was being manipulated.[6] Hoffmann-La Roche demanded that Stanley Adams, a British citizen, be arrested for "industrial espionage"! More incredible still, the company got its way, and Adams went to prison. His wife, the mother of three children, killed herself. What was the Department of Trade doing all this time? After all, it is their job to see that the 1972 agreements are kept. They stood firmly behind Hoffmann-La Roche throughout.

The efficiency of Hoffmann-La Roche is an example to all. One need only note how, after the Seveso disaster of July-August 1976, Adolf W. Jann,[7] the managing director of the company, disclaimed the company's responsibility—even though the toxic dioxin gas spreading over the countryside and damaging human beings came right out of his own chimneys![8]

In the valium affair, which I have just mentioned, the company behaved in much the same way. It briefed as its lawyer Maître Claudius Alder, National Councillor and leader of the Independent Party. This stabilized the political situation: any questions raised in Parliament about valium were simply buried in the files of the Federal Government. There remained the mass media – and one would have expected a television team from Zürich to broadcast a critical documentary about Jann. They did: the programme was called "The Audit", and Hoffmann-La Roche sued the reporters, the cameraman, the soundman and the producer for libel. On 8 June 1976, the EEC Commission gave judgment in favour of Stanley Adams, and fined Hoffmann-La Roche 900,000 Swiss francs. But inside Switzerland, Hoffmann-La Roche remained omnipotent. A few days after the Brussels verdict, Stanley Adams was tried and found guilty by the Basle court, condemned to twelve months in gaol, five years' exclusion from the country and a 25,000 franc fine.

Nor is Hoffmann-La Roche the only Swiss multinational to behave in this way. Nestlé-Alimentana, the world's largest producer of baby-foods, powdered milk and instant coffee, uses the same expeditious methods to confound its critics. Consider how Nestlé behaves abroad: in Peru, the Nestlé empire has established a holding company which in turn controls a number of food-processing firms. This holding company is called Perulac. It stands out among the American, German and French multinationals in Peru – none of which is famed for treating its labour force particularly kindly – for the extremely harsh conditions and low pay it gives its workers. In 1971, the Perulac workers went on strike. Nestlé refused to negotiate and the police were finally sent in. All trade union militants, all the workers' delegates and negotiators were arrested and vanished into military prisons. A group of workers thereupon appealed to the international trade union of food industry workers whose general secretariat is in Geneva. The general secretary sent a representative to Lima. He was detained and deported from Peru.

Nestlé is equally effective when it comes to muzzling critics at home. In 1974, the English organization War on Want, which is specially concerned with children, published a pamphlet showing how Nestlé employees, dressed as nurses, dissuade mothers in the Third World from breast-feeding their babies, and talk them into buying artificial substitutes – the resulting malnutrition causing the children to suffer from mental and physical deficiencies. The pamphlet was translated into French (it was entitled "Nestlé kills babies") by thirteen young people in the "Third World Group". Nestlé filed no fewer than five criminal suits against them – for damage to its reputation, financial loss, etc. The Berne court found the thirteen guilty on 24 June 1976. They then lodged an appeal. It was rejected.

I repeat: in the Hoffmann-La Roche affair, and the Nestlé affair, and in other, similar cases when a multinational company faces criticism at home or abroad, the Department of Trade, instinctively it seems, sides with the multinational. One cannot help wondering *why* there should be such spontaneous and effective solidarity between it and the giants.

All I can attempt here is phenomenological analysis: structural analysis would be very difficult. However, a few indications spring to the eye. For one thing, there is a constant exchange of personnel between the oligarchy and the Trade Department. Rothenbuehler, the executive secretary of Vorort, was appointed trade delegate in charge of the Latin American section. His departure from the industrialists' body coincided with a move in the opposite direction by a section director from the Department of Trade—Veyrassat became secretary of Vorort. In 1976, the director general of Nestlé in Austria, Peter C. Bettschart, was appointed a trade delegate with ambassadorial rank. Another point is that before any major international negotiation, there is a complicated procedure known as "consultation"—which is a way of letting the oligarchy express, and all too often impose, their point of view. Again, since the Second World War a permanent economic delegation has been in existence (with no basis in law) in which the oligarchy play a decisive part: its job is to lay the ground for the economic decisions, both domestic and foreign, of the Federal Council.

True, differences can arise between the Department of Trade and the oligarchy. Peter Nobel has analysed their respective standpoints in international negotiations in some detail, and one of the chapters in his study is cautiously entitled: "Possibilities of conflict between the state and the multinationals".[9] He quotes the occasion in GATT, during the awkward Kennedy Round negotiations, when the head of the Swiss delegation and some of his colleagues found themselves in opposition to the directors of the multinational Sandoz company (chemicals and pharmaceuticals). The Swiss government wanted Sandoz to change the trading practice of its subsidiary in the United States, which was embarrassing Switzerland in a difficult tariff and trade negotiation with the government in Washington. Sandoz refused, but eventually gave way to some extent. However, my readers may rest assured that such conflicts will not arise in future: Hans Schoffner, who was then federal Minister of the Economy, and formerly a director of the Department of Trade, is today vice-president of the Sandoz management board.

Of course it is absolutely natural – and indeed necessary – for a sovereign state to defend the material interests of its citizens abroad, including those of bankers, industrialists and arms dealers. But what takes place every day in Switzerland is a different matter altogether. Instead of the necessary defence of the interests of all, there is a narrow but effective defence of specific privileges. The state has become simply an intermediary, and often even an instrument, of imperialist aggression. What the Federal Council says and what the majority of the population want – the oft-stated policy of active neutrality – is no more than a verbal formula. It bears no relation at all to the day-to-day reality of Swiss foreign policy.

The second element in this colonization of foreign policy by merchant banks and multinational corporations is rather harder to identify. The following diagram, which I have taken from Keel,[10] is useful:

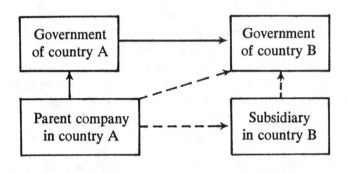

$$Direct\ action\ \ -\ -\ -\ -\ -\ -$$
$$Indirect\ action\ \ \ \text{———————}$$

If we analyse it sector by sector we see that this is how it works: the secondary imperialist oligarchy exercise considerable power in a number of the states on the periphery (and indeed also at the centre). They can therefore get the governments of those countries to make demands upon the Swiss government to suit their own interest. For example: the ADELA (Atlantic Community Development Group for Latin America) financial empire, run by a coalition of Swiss and foreign merchant banks, operates in Latin America. I was able to check for myself the "effects" of the ADELA's policy in Paraguay. ADELA came to Paraguay four years ago. It bought up CAPSA (Companía Algodonera Paraguaya SA), and CAPSA/ ADELA today controls over 80 per cent of the soya market in Paraguay. Its factories also process cocoa, cotton and sunflower seeds. Soya and its derivatives are the principal product of the small and middle peasants of Paraguay; about 75 per cent of the marketable value of agricultural production (apart from dairy produce) comes from soya. Some 140,000 tonnes are produced per year, and are exported to the rest of Latin America, to Asia, and to Europe. ADELA owns three major factories – producing oil and margarine, and transforming the waste products into animal foodstuffs – and has a virtual monopoly of exporting soya, vegetable oil and derivatives.

But CAPSA/ADELA has efficient ways of continuing to enlarge its empire. In the Pirapoa area, where several thousand

With practical help from the three great Swiss banks and various large industrial enterprises, private banks for aiding development have come into being and operate in the developing countries with capital provided by large European, American and Japanese companies. Sifida (International Finance Company for Investment and Development in Africa) operates in Africa. When it was set up in 1970, the three major Swiss banks took 50 million dollars' worth of preferred shares (12.5 million in paid-up shares), along with the IFC and the Bank for Aid to African Development. The whole venture was co-ordinated by Crédit Suisse.

In 1968, the PICA (Private Investment Company for Asia) was set up, and Swiss banks and industries also bought shares in that.

The most longstanding institution of this kind, however, is the Atlantic Community Development Group for Latin America (ADELA). Among its Swiss members are the three major banks, as well as André SA, Volkart Bros., Ciba-Geigy, Elektro-Watt, Motor-Columbus, Nestlé, Bührle, Sulzer, Hoffmann-La Roche and Holderbank. "In seven and a half years, ADELA has increased its assets from 16 million dollars to 300 million, and by the way it has used its capital has generated many times that sum in investments. In the past financial year the interest rate has risen to 8.1 per cent of the capital invested (*Neue Zürcher Zeitung*, 9 February 1973). Private companies for aiding "development" function as bridgeheads in the Third World. They have to experiment, and they pool experiences: "Shares in ADELA are only given to healthy businesses certain of making a profit" (H.Hofer). During the first five and a half years of its activity, ADELA got things going and attracted something like 400 million dollars in share investment from private firms in the Third World. It also has its own specialized subsidiaries: Adelatec (Technical and Management Services Co. SA), Adeltrade (Trade and Development Co. SA), and finally AAF (Assessores financieiros SA).

(from Kappeler, *op.cit.*)

Japanese immigrants work as small farmers,[11] a Japanese company planned to build a vegetable oil factory to use the soya planted by the Japanese community (at a better price to the grower). So CAPSA/ADELA built a factory nearby which adopted a policy of buying at very high prices indeed. The Japanese firm could not compete. Once the Japanese community project had been killed, CAPSA/ADELA then shut down its factory and departed.

CAPSA/ADELA's method is as follows: the peasants start to sell their soya in April, and the Paraguayan government then fix a mandatory purchase price. In April 1974, the government fixed a price of 21 guaranís a kilo. CAPSA/ADELA would not buy at that price, and demanded that it be reduced to 16 guaranís. The peasants went home again, with their sacks of soya still piled up on their ox-carts. The classic scenario then unfolded precisely as it had for four years. Weeks passed, and the farmers' slender financial resources were used up. If CAPSA/ADELA did not buy by August, they would starve. Since soya had become virtually the only crop grown by thousands of peasants, they had to buy most of their food (cassava, sugar, wheat, flour, etc.). In 1974, as in the preceding years, CAPSA/ADELA held out, and the government gave way – and so did the peasants: they sold their soya at the price dictated by the company, 16 guaranís a kilo. (There is in addition another form of oppression: not only does ADELA dictate the purchasing price of soya but it also has a monopoly of selling soya oil in Paraguay. The selling price of a litre of oil was 110 guaranís in 1974. It takes 5 kilos of soya, at 16 guaranís per kilo, to make a litre of oil.)

The directors of ADELA, who have enormous influence with the Paraguayan government, have a strong social sense. Naturally moved by the plight of the small peasants, of agricultural workers and the jobless, they suggested to General Stroessner that he ask Switzerland for aid. Thus the Confederation – i.e. the Swiss taxpayer – came to finance a vast programme of technical aid in Paraguay. No fewer than four aid and development projects are now under way: an animal foodstuffs factory in Minga Guazu, to help the small farmers and pig-breeders in the east; two training schools, one for forestry workers, the other for apprentice mechanics; the fourth, and most important of all, is a huge project comprising a school for training people to run co-operatives, an agricultural school, a domestic science school, an industrial sawmill, model farms and a stock-breeding scheme using imported livestock. All these undertakings are in the Pastorea area, near Encarnación. Their object is to assist the 30,000 or so tenant farmers, landless peasants and their families, deported by the Stroessner government – with neither training nor equipment – to the virgin forest of the Alta Paraná. All these Swiss schemes are intended to overcome the desperate poverty of the Paraguayan peasants – which is indeed desperate, but has actually been caused by ADELA, a subsidiary of the great Swiss banks! [12]

To take another example: the Lima Light and Power Company, a powerful Swiss monopoly controlling the energy industry in the Lima district of Peru, built a series of barrages and power stations in the Andean foothills of central Peru during the fifties. To do this involved transplanting a mass of peasants and semi-skilled workers, persuading them to leave their homes and in some cases their small plots of land. By the middle sixties, the building work was complete, and the labour force were left jobless. Rather than accept-

Various Swiss firms operating in the Third World conceived the idea of financing their investment programme with the kindly and effective help of funds from the World Bank. For example, a whole series of finance companies have been involved since the last century in financing new clients by way of subsidiary companies in order to open new outlets for electrical equipment. Sudelektra (South American Electricity Company) finances power stations in Peru. Its Peruvian subsidiaries, Lima Light and Hidradina, enjoy considerable privileges, since a special Peruvian law allows them to make a tax-free profit of 8.5 per cent, and pay only 3 per cent tax on the rest; in exchange for which the companies are committed to increasing their production capacity by 10 per cent per year. The Sudelektra management consultant, Kohn, of Motor-Columbus, noted that "The transfer of dividends, interest and repayments has worked well, despite sweeping currency restrictions and stringent transfer regulations". What is interesting about this is the fact that of a total of 925 million francs invested in Sudelektra, 525 million represent shares issued in dollars and Swiss francs. 290 million of this comes from the World Bank, and the rest (around 230 million) either directly by the Sudelektra group or indirectly via the Swiss capital market. Thus the World Bank has provided over half the foreign capital invested in Sudelektra, and 30 per cent of the total share capital of 925 million francs. Sudelektra has for a long time been paying its private shareholders in Switzerland a dividend of 12 per cent.

The Compañía Italo-Argentina (CIA) is another member of the finance group that gravitates around Motor-Columbus. Like Sudelektra in Peru, it is legally allowed 8 per cent of net profit (after repayment of capital) by the Argentinian government. In 1969, the CIA received a loan of 15.8 million dollars from the Inter-American Aid to Development Bank (one of whose four major money brokers is Switzerland) for expanding its installations, as well as having received a credit of 42 million francs in 1966 from a consortium of Swiss banks. A further 45 million in credits from Swiss banks went to the Industrial Bank of Argentina. The money was used to buy Swiss merchandise, including a 250 Kw turbine system, the largest in South America. The *Bulletin de la Société de banque suisse* (no. 3, 1967) talks of "appreciable financial aid" — by which it means financial transactions supported by the Inter-American Bank and guaranteed by the Argentinian and Swiss governments.

Large Swiss firms have managed to get credits from the World Bank to use for their "normal" trading activities. This leads to a kind of closed circuit for the insulated circulation of Swiss capital through the countries of the Third World. Swiss capital is channelled from our banks into the World Bank; most World Bank credits are used to buy Swiss industrial goods. It is solely the Swiss economy, and not that of the developing country, that benefits from the credits given by the World Bank. When the new installations start to operate, the profits they make in the developing country must be used to pay interest to Switzerland — so most of it simply vanishes. If throughout the period of the loan the installations financed by it bring a return of 15 per cent on the capital invested (which is a high estimate), the 6 or 8 per cent interest swallows up half of it. To say nothing of the cost of replacing equipment as it wears out. In fifteen years, annual payments of 6 to 8 per cent will have mounted up to at least 90 per cent of the initial loan; then, unless an extension has been granted, the loan falls due. So, in addition to paying interest and the cost of upkeep, money must be put aside during those fifteen years to repay the loan; in other words, a sinking fund (which includes a further 6 per cent of the initial sum). All that is left in the developing country, once the loan has been paid back, is a fifteen-year-old installation.

(Kappeler, *op. cit.*)

ing any responsibility for this major social problem and trying to find other ways of employing them, the Swiss managing director of Lima Light and Power, a M. Mariotti, approached the Peruvian government – who turned to Switzerland for aid! The Swiss government sent millions of francs, a number of experts, and supplies of cattle and machinery to the Peruvian government, to aid in resettling, feeding, educating and providing work for the men, women and children uprooted by the building activities of Lima Light and Power.

One final example is that of Motor-Columbus, an important firm of industrial consultants. Motor-Columbus proposed an industrial development plan for Ecuador. The plan was requested by the Ecuador government, but the fees received by Motor-Columbus were paid to the tune of two million Swiss francs by the Service de la Co-opération Technique – i.e. the Swiss taxpayer. When the plan was ready, it just so happened that a Swiss consortium was able to undertake the largest project, the construction of a waterworks – at very profitable terms. The government of Ecuador, "informed" and guided by Motor-Columbus, then concluded a bilateral outline agreement for technical co-operation with Switzerland.

Another dimension of this pseudo-neutrality is worth looking at. Since the International Labour Organization came into being in Geneva, it has formulated 143 international agreements concerning the freedom of trade unions, job security, wage parity, and hygiene in factories. Only 31 of them have ever been ratified by the Swiss government. If a Swiss citizen commits a crime abroad, he is subject to penal law. But the multinational companies whose headquarters are in Switzerland can do things abroad that are contrary both to Swiss law and to international agreements to which Switzerland is party, and have nothing to fear. The fact of having signed such agreements means that the Confederation is committed to seeing that its citizens do not break them, yet the Confederation almost never takes any action.[13]

Another chapter, perhaps the most tragic of all, in this history is written from day to day by those who trade in armaments. The death industry is an essential activity of all the secondary imperialisms. In Switzerland it falls into three different categories:

The large Swiss consultant-engineering firms have expanded their activities in the Third World enormously. The Vorort enquiry into the Swiss economy and European interdependence points out that the main field of operations of those firms is in the Third World. These operations must be included in our study, because their profits often take the form of "invisible earnings" – like the profits of banks and insurance companies. Such firms do not primarily exist to sell plant and equipment, but rather to make their technological skill available for the construction of a particular installation, or the manufacture of a particular product. Unfortunately, they function in the same kind of insulated circuit as I have described: their expertise comes from outside, from Swiss schools and laboratories; that expertise is brought into the country by Swiss people, and leads to greater profits flowing *out* of the developing country. As instances of the activity of Swiss engineering companies, one may cite the surveys for electrical installations in Taiwan made by Elektro- Watt and the Société Générale pour l'Industrie (financed by the Asian Development Bank), or the Venezuelan order for a powerful electric generator from Motor-Columbus. Swiss engineering firms are also busy in Anbarli, in Turkey. In most cases, their activity results in large orders being placed with Swiss industry. The Suiselektra plant in South America was planned by the Banque des Chemins de Fer and Motor-Columbus – which meant that all the orders were certain to go to Swiss firms. ... According to Tibor Mende, consultant-engineering companies, which are today becoming one of the major forms of international monopoly competition, wield a *de facto* control over the structures of investment, and prevent their being adapted to a country's existing production capacities, or so co-ordinated as to organize the local production of equipment. In 1967, this sector was making a profit of just under 500 million francs per year. With an annual increase of 20 per cent (disapproved by UNCTAD) it must now be over a billion.

(Kappeler, *op. cit.*)

(1) There are the international dealers who use Switzerland as the rear-base or logistical centre of their operations. From their discreet offices in the rue de Mont-Blanc in Geneva, or their chalets in Gstaad, they buy, sell, transport and re-sell armaments that never actually touch Swiss soil. What Switzerland contributes is the telex, the duty-free airports, the transport facilities, the numbered bank accounts, and the offices. Since only Swiss manufactures and exports are subject to authorization, so long as the armaments do not themselves pass through Switzerland, any bank or any individual dealer can buy, sell and re-sell all the weaponry of war from Geneva,

Lausanne or Zürich. For example: several deputies were astounded to find that Samuel Cummings, the managing director of Interarmco, Monaco, the largest private armaments dealer in the world,[14] could spend several months of every year living in his chalet at Villars-sur-Ollon. The Federal Council were fully aware that he was there, but no action was ever taken against Cummings. It is hard to believe that some business was not conducted from his chalet.

2. There is a second category of arms dealers who also present all the elements of respectability. These are the great multinational and multiproduct companies of foreign origin, but with their headquarters in Zürich or Geneva. For example, the world's largest manufacturer of napalm, the Dow Chemical Corporation, has its main office outside America in Zürich. It owns four separate "Swiss" companies, independently financed and managed.[15] All the sales of napalm outside the United States are arranged, invoiced and paid for by the office in Zürich. Honeywell is another example. This company is the world's largest manufacturer of anti-personnel weapons (fragmentation bombs and landmines, etc.). Every day, somewhere in the world, children, men and women die, burnt by napalm or torn to shreds by fragmentation bombs. Two million children died that way between 1968 and 1971 in Vietnam.[16] On two separate occasions the Federal Council was called upon to consider what could be done, and each time it declared that it could "do nothing", either against Dow Chemical in Zürich or against Honeywell in Geneva.[17]

(3) The third category consists of the Swiss multinational armaments firms. There are really only two of them. First the empire of the amazing Dieter Bührle, the well-bred son of a most unusual merchant. The father was one of the largest arms suppliers during the Second World War; he was also a cultured humanist, who assembled the largest private collection of French Impressionist paintings in Europe. The empire he bequeathed to his son covers three continents. In Switzerland its most important branches are the original Oerlikon company (in the suburbs of Zürich) and the Hispano company (in Geneva). The Bührle empire specializes in machine-guns, tank guns and turrets. The other homegrown multinational company is Sig-Schaffouse, which manufactures automatic rifles.

These companies are virtually unassailable – for various reasons. In the first place, they manufacture all the weapons used by the Swiss army, at terms entirely dictated by themselves; thus they can claim to be working for "the national good". In the second place, they have enormous financial power – their profits appear to be truly astronomical.[18] In fact, they benefit from a quite peculiar set of circumstances: Bührle, Contraves and Sig-Schaffouse make very few heavy weapons; they specialize in infantry weapons – automatic rifles, anti-aircraft guns, anti-personnel mines. Swiss firms even have a world monopoly of certain products – for instance, Pilatus aircraft needing twenty-five to thirty metres of runway for take-off. Apart from the war in the Middle East, the only wars, internal repressions and punitive expeditions in which such arms and munitions are used in any quantity are conflicts between (or within) the unstable, continually trouble-torn nations of the Third World. Their leaders seldom have the money to pay for B-52s or aircraft-carriers; however, they buy impressive quantities of the sort of light arms that troops with very little training can handle easily. On 8 October 1967, Ernesto Che Guevara was killed at Higueras in Bolivia by a Swiss automatic rifle. The Bolivian Rangers were equipped with these guns by Sig-Schaffouse in 1966, after the Barrientos/Sig agreement had been ratified by the Federal Council. The same weapon is today in the hands of the *boinas negras*, the Chilean army corps whose special function is executing workers, students and peasants "trying to escape".[19]

I have always found the farce of Swiss pseudo-neutrality absolutely astonishing. I never tire of listening to interminable speeches in parliament by our Foreign Minister about "interdependence", and international "solidarity". They have all the poetic unreality of lies told out of ignorance or naivety. Unfortunately, these lies kill people.

1. This institution fulfils the function of a Ministry of Foreign Trade in Switzerland.
2. *Vorort* is the German name, also used by French and Italian speakers, for the Swiss employers' organization.
3. Paul-Rodolphe Jollès, director of the Department of Trade.
4. Philippe de Weck, general manager of the Union Bank of Switzerland.
5. To understand the Confederation's foreign trade policy, see Appendix I to this chapter, taken from Hollenstein.
6. For a detailed analysis of the affair cf. *Le Monde,* 22 March 1975.
7. Cf. Part I, Chapter 2, p. 00.
8. Cf. the interview with Jann in *Der Blick,* Zürich, 6 August 1976.
9. Nobel, *op. cit.*
10. Keel-Nguyen, *op. cit.*
11. Stockbreeding is the preserve of four landowning families and the foreign companies, who control between them most of the land. For instance, the British multinational company Liebig alone possesses almost 15 per cent of the land in Paraguay.
12. The management of ADELA are not without irony. Their man in Paraguay is a certain Mr Fischer, who was previously an expert commissioned by the Swiss government to organize a farming and stockbreeding co-operative at Jenaro-Herrera in Peru.
13. For the social, economic and political effects of private Swiss industries in the dependent countries, see Appendix II to this chapter, taken from Strahm.
14. *Time,* 3 March 1975.
15. Cf. the commercial register of the canton of Zürich.
16. See the report of the United States Senate sub-committee for refugees by Edward Kennedy, Congressional Publications, June 1971.
17. Cf. the government's replies to questions from Jean Ziegler in the National Council, 28 June 1972 and 12 December 1973.
18. The Swiss armaments industry refuses to publish complete accounts of its expenditure or its profits, on grounds of military secrecy. In the United States, on the other hand, arms firms are obliged to make their accounts public, and it is noteworthy that their profits are far higher than those of comparable civilian industries: 17.5 per cent as against an average of 10.6 per cent. Cf. Delay *et al., Documentation pour l'initiative contre l'exportation d'armes,* Geneva, 1972.
19. Arms exports are continually going up. They amounted to 236 million francs in 1974, and 369 million in 1976 (an increase of 133 million). Most of them go to repressive dictatorships: in 1975 the largest customer was Iran, and the second largest Spain. South Africa is also a very good customer. In theory there is a federal law regulating the export and manufacture of war materials. But the law tends to be ineffective: transit markets are found – such as Singapore – from where arms can be re-sold to countries to which it is illegal to sell direct.

Appendix to Chapter 8

(The aggressive and far from neutral nature of Swiss foreign policy becomes especially clear when one analyses the policy of foreign trade and of private investment by finance capital in the Third World. I quote here first an analysis of the former by Hollenstein, then one of the latter by Strahm. J.Z.)

I. The policy of foreign trade

The facts are as follows : [1]

(1) The developing countries derive over 80 per cent of their export earnings from selling raw materials, whose prices – for various reasons – rise more slowly than the prices of manufactured products (thus the whole problem of "terms of trade"). Since increased consumption, especially of agricultural products, is strictly limited, the only way to increase returns is by exporting more; but this can only be done if industrial countries abandon the practice of protecting their own agriculture.

(2) Given that there is a limit to the increased consumption of raw materials, given also their relative fall in value, and the unilateral production left over from colonial days, it is essential for the developing countries to export more manufactured goods. But this can only happen if markets are opened to Third World products in the industrialized countries, and new outlets are created for them.

(3) The trend for terms of trade to go down, together with huge fluctuations in the prices of raw materials, impose heavy losses on the developing countries which it is important to reduce or counterbalance.

Even though the Swiss tariff system is more generous than those of the great European powers and Japan (the USA has as yet made no concession in the matter of preferences : this is called "burden sharing"), it is not easy for imports of manufactured products from the developing countries to rise.

The reasons are as follows :

(1) Industrialization in the developing countries would be easier and faster if it began in a sector of production related to agriculture – food products for example. Unfortunately, it is very unusual for duty to be reduced on foodstuffs, and when it is, it is always in specific cases, generally of merchandise that is not in competition with any Swiss product. Furthermore, for such products better rates have often been granted to the member states of the European Free Trade Association (EFTA, to which Switzerland

147

still belongs). Thus, most of the developing countries are excluded in advance from the benefits of preferential tariffs.

(2) The Free Trade agreement between Switzerland and the Common Market[2] reduced the amount of preference given to manufactures exported by the developing countries.[3] Owing to the more competitive European free trade, the European market was to become the scene of increased competition, which could only reduce the value of price agreements proposed earlier by the developing countries. Then, further regulations – above all the principle of added value – have led to more division of labour in Europe, even at the expense of supposedly developing countries. It is in fact more profitable to buy "pre-products" from other European states, since only then can the overall manufacture (the added value) be described as "Swiss made" and so be able to be exported duty-free to the European community.[4] Thus any tendency to put raw materials through the early stages of processing in the developing countries is discouraged. The free trade areas have made considerable changes in trade patterns,[5] and the Third World countries are suffering the effects. It seems extraordinarily optimistic to expect European integration to achieve so much growth that the ill-effects will be entirely overcome by a huge increase in European demand for goods from the developing countries.[6]

(3) Markets rendered more accessible by a reduction of tariffs are, of course, a necessary condition, but by no means the only one, for an increase of imports from the developing countries: those countries want to be able to explore new possibilities for exporting. "It is up to them", says the Federal Council.[7] "They must create an investment climate so attractive that foreign firms *have* to bring in funds." So marketing and the creation of new outlets are also the developing countries' own responsibility.

Here is a provisional conclusion:

Because export goods (potentially of enormous importance for the countries of the Third World) are subject to tariff laws, because European free trade has reduced the role of preferential tariffs, and because there has been no consistent attempt to enable the developing countries to derive the maximum benefit from the system, it is probable that their exports will ultimately gain only the most minute advantage from preferential tariffs.

The problem of marketing raw materials – particularly agricultural produce – is in turn bound up with the problem of terms of trade. The first thing to be said is that, given the very slight increase in consumption, the only way imports of raw materials from the developing countries can be substantially increased is by abandoning agrarian protectionism in the industrial countries, including Switzerland. It can then be seen that a fall in the price of primary agricultural products affects the Swiss farmer as much as it affects all but a privileged minority of the people in the developing countries. Large fluctuations in the price of raw materials make rational economic planning impossible.

If we are to resolve all these problems so as to assist *international* development, order must be established gradually on the basis of the following principles:

(1) There must be a system of international agreements to stabilize the prices of raw materials at a level fixed in accordance with supply and demand.

(2) Agrarian protectionism must gradually be abolished, and at the same time the developing countries must be given a larger share of the market; this should be arranged by an agreement about raw materials (market sharing approach).[8]

These two measures depend on one important condition: that the producers of the raw materials can be assured of a certain return, independent of pricing policies. Therefore:

(3) In the industrial nations, farmers should be guaranteed a return by direct allowances; in the developing countries, producers of raw materials should be paid adequate compensation to make up for what they lose by any deterioration in the terms of trade.

(Hollenstein, *op. cit.*)

II. Foreign private investment and the poor countries[9]

a. Effects on public prosperity

Argument. Private investments are productive – that is to say, they increase both the production of merchandise and the national product. Consequently estimates of profitability by private investors offer the best possible guarantee that resources will be used productively.

Objection. An increase in the production of goods in national economies where the majority of the population are in extreme deprivation is certainly not a negligible factor. Development, after all, implies making available a large quantity of useful products. But the problem is to know which products seem useful, and to whom. Economists have their own terms for describing public prosperity: the gross national product, for instance, says almost everything as far as they are concerned: the commercial value of production and services is added up, and made the yardstick for industrial and agricultural production. Yet it is obvious that the usual definition of the gross national product bears no relation whatever to the quality of life.[10]

Private investments are not a factor for prosperity simply by the fact of "working" profitably for the investors. The private businessman's cost-benefit analysis is by no means identical with any cost-benefit analysis that might be made from the community's point of view. What appears profitable to the entrepreneur in terms of his own private economy may not be so at all in terms of the public economy.

It is only in very recent years that any kind of cost-benefit analysis has been attempted from the point of view of the community.[11] Any industrial project may engender costs that are borne not by the industrialist but by the community: the expenses of the infrastructure – traffic, energy, schools, housing – possible tax reductions, effects on the ecological system, and so on.[12] It is not scientifically possible to reckon up all the effects in terms of monetary value: this is a political matter, and in the last analysis any assessment of its demands or the damage it does must be made by whoever holds power.

Swiss firms which, as a general rule, take little account of the social cost of their operations, are reluctant to part with any information. Here is a typical instance of the negligence of capitalism over the harmful effects that can be caused by setting up private industrial installations. A director of Sandoz describes a new project in Pakistan:

> In this underdeveloped country, with its aridity and lack of vegetation, one seldom finds so many advantages coexisting in one place: the relative proximity of Karachi with its international harbour and airport . . . , good communications, the proximity of the Indus for water supplies, the bed of a small river nearby into which the water can be drawn off. Industrial water, purified in an ordinary domestic filtration plant, together with the cooling water and other water carrying chemicals, can all then drain away into an expansion chamber from which it will evaporate in the usual way. During the short and violent rainy season the process has to be modified, and the expansion chamber overflows into drains that have been dug to carry the water, so that it is properly dispersed. However it is planned to construct our own system of pipes, and sooner or later a purifying plant for used water with a conduit to carry it to the Indus.[13]

When one recalls that the Indus provides water for the day-to-day needs of a vast population, it becomes obvious that for a large plant not to purify and return the water it uses represents a real loss of amenity for the poorer sectors of the population. This is a good example of the fact that estimates of profitability which do not refer to the social cost are no yardstick for measuring the prosperity of the community as a whole. If the social cost be counted, one would find that a great many "profitable" industrial projects are in fact large loss-makers. In relation to the above-mentioned project in Pakistan, if we suppose that the water taken for industry is worth no more than one centime per litre, and that the factory uses one cubic metre of industrial water per minute, then the social cost, merely in terms of pollution, would amount to 5.2 million francs – perhaps almost as much as the income of the factory.

b. Effect on employment

Argument. Private investment creates job opportunities in the developing countries, therefore has a beneficial effect on development. *Objection.* I do not deny that this is true. Far from it. However, the argument is not convincing by itself as stated. One has to consider not just how many workers are earning their living in a new foreign firm, but, more important, how many workers have *lost* jobs over the years as this particular sector of production became industrialized, and the assembly line replaced the craftsman – and how many more will lose them in future.

In a great many of the developing countries, textiles, foodstuffs and consumer goods were being produced at craft level before there was any investment by foreign industry. It is not uncommon to find that the streamlined, expensive techniques of industrial production have made as many – or more – workers employed in craft production redundant as they are employing in their new factories, to say nothing of inhibiting the development of future craft manufacture, which would have employed far more workers than highly mechanized industry.[14]

An example from the dairy industry illustrates this very clearly. In the Mexican state of Chiapas – one and a half times the size of Switzerland, and with 1.6 million inhabitants – Nestlé have set up a plant for processing milk (pasteurization and cheese-making). For a total investment of some 60 million pesos (20 million Swiss francs), work is provided for 89 permanent workers and 92 seasonal ones.[15] Is it worth it? The factory, the only one of its kind in Chiapas state, collects a large proportion of the state's milk production. Given this costly production structure plus high local unemployment, one cannot help wondering whether a more modest programme would not have been more liable to help development. A few hundred ordinary cheese-dairies would probably have brought more substantial economic benefits to the people of Chiapas.[16] The Nestlé company's powerful position in the market seems certain to prevent the establishment of small co-operative cheese-making enterprises in the state.

It must be pointed out that the sort of industrial development offered them by the advanced technology of the industrial countries can only be achieved by the developing countries at the cost of heavy sacrifices. Between 1970 and 1980, 226 million people of working age have been looking for jobs in the Third World.[17] According to the statistics for unemployment, 20 to 40 per cent of the active population today are unemployed or underemployed. This means the Third World would need more jobs to be created in ten years than Europe and the US combined could produce.

In Switzerland, it costs on average some 60,000 francs to create an industrial job. Even reckoning on a lower initial cost for the developing countries, say 10,000 francs,[18] if we multiply that by 200 million, we arrive at the astronomical sum of 2,000 billion francs – to continue along the path of industrial development, that is to say. In ten years that is unthinkable. Since it is to be expected that, in a case of large-scale industrialization, a proportion of the farming population (who are today still 60-80 per cent of the active population) will leave the primary sector, one must reckon on still more jobs being needed.

c. Private profits

Argument. The idea that profit-making is the most characteristic effect of private investment in the developing countries is almost a commonplace, yet it is open to question.

Objection. There is no point in arguing about the profit figures, since the multinational trusts have so many different ways of manipulating the figures they provide. Here are some of them:

(i) Estimating the capital value of the investment, upon which the profit margin must be based, is an arbitrary matter. The investor himself determines the value of the funds he has brought into the developing country.[19]

(ii) Internal movements of money within a multinational trust that relate to internal transfers of merchandise can be concealed by falsifying prices. Profits may be minimized on the books by underestimating the output and overestimating the input. By underestimating the price of the merchandise sent from the subsidiary in the developing country to the parent company in Switzerland, restrictions on profit-transfers can be evaded and tax liability shifted from one country to the other.[20]

(iii) High royalties and consultation fees for technological know-how can be used to cover up transfers of profits. It is not unusual for the major contribution of the investing company to consist in providing specialist skills (patents, plans, industrial procedures) while the bulk of the money to finance the venture comes from the developing country.[21] Since the price set on technological exchange is quite arbitrary, shares in profits can be taken out of the country by that means even though they may have been earned with local capital.

(iv) Profits can be masked by high rates of amortization. (In certain countries, "amortization" can also cover restocking of raw materials.)

(v) Tax concessions and investment privileges are also forms of profit. With a new type of dual taxation agreement with the developing countries, Switzerland enables Swiss investors to make substantial tax savings.[22]

Such ingenuity in scheming and fraud makes it clear that one must maintain a cautious reserve when studying the profit figures put out by the companies themselves. In the case of Swiss subsidiaries in developing countries, it must be admitted that manipulation more often takes place at the bottom than at the top, since Switzerland is a country with relatively low taxes and it is therefore well worth arranging to pay tax at the Swiss end. In some US companies the opposite is the case: they try to earn as much as possible in some developing countries and declare their gross profits there (particularly in the oil industry) because the tax rates in the USA are higher.

Swiss firms tend to give very little information about the profits they make from their investments in the developing countries. Up to a point we know the average profits of such investments earned by firms in the United States (in 1967, 13 per cent), in England (in 1966, 10 per cent excluding oil) and in the German Federal Republic (6.3 per cent excluding mining and chemicals). The levels of reinvestment amounted to 18 per cent for US subsidiaries, 34 per cent for English, and 70 per cent for German.[23] The lower profit rates of German investors are due to the low maturity level of their investments.[24] From the point of view of the developing countries, the result of the western companies thus removing their profits is a considerable loss of capital which seriously upsets their balance of payments. In Latin America especially, where investment has been going on for a long time, this transferring of profits has a very damaging effect on the economy.[25]

As for private Swiss investment in the Third World, it causes a notable degree of decapitalization. It is certainly not an over-estimate to say that, in 1971, repatriated profits from direct Swiss investment amounted to a total of 185 million Swiss francs. During that year, officially declared new investment was 270 million Swiss francs: this figure includes profits ploughed back, even though they do not in fact represent any transfer of capital into the developing countries.[26] Of the 270 million francs invested, my estimate is that 127 million were profits reinvested; thus only about 143 million were new investments – i.e. money that actually went from Switzerland to the Third World.

In Latin America, however, the sums repatriated are higher than the new investments. In 1971 profits of about 119 million Swiss francs were transferred from Swiss investments in Latin America. Only 102 million francs were invested that year, more than half of which were residual profits made inside Latin America.[27]

(Strahm, *op. cit.*)

1. L.B.Pearson *et al.*, "The Pearson Report", UN document, 1969.
2. Part of the agreement between the Swiss Confederation and the European Community. For the text of the agreement and additional material, cf. *Message du Conseil fédéral à l'assemblee fédérale*, 16 August 1972, Berne.
3. The removal of tariffs within the EEC was scheduled to take place in five stages, each of 20 per cent, from 1973 to 1977.
4. "Service d'information Tiers Monde", Bulletin no. 13, 21 November 1972, Berne.
5. See for instance "Enquête du secrétariat AELE", *NZZ* no. 291, 25 June 1972.
6. See UNCTAD, TD/B/C 5/8, *Effects of the Enlargement of the European Economic Community on the Generalized System of Preferences*, 1973.
7. Reply of the Federal Council to a question from National Councillor Müller-Marzohl on encouraging imports, 6 October 1972.
8. See UNCTAD, TD/99, *The International Development Strategy in Action/The Role of UNCTAD*, report by the secretary general of UNCTAD, February 1972.
9. R.H.Strahm, "Critères de jugement de l'effet de développement des investissements privés dans les pays en voie de développement", *Les Investissements privés suisses*, Geneva (Institut universitaire des hautes études internationales), pp.60-97.
10. We are at last coming to understand that the Gross Domestic Product is not necessarily an indicator of prosperity. For instance, if I have a car accident, I increase the GDP by the cost of repairing my car and the amount I pay the hospital. If I put a franc in a parking metre, I increase the GDP by one franc. A woman working in a factory increases the GDP, whereas a woman staying at home to bring up her children is not productive at all, economically speaking.
11. In the economic literature of the world, there are only two comprehensive works on this subject: I.M.D.Little and I.A.Mirrless, *Manual of Industrial Project Evaluation in Developing Countries, Social-Cost-Benefit-Analysis*, vol. II, OECD, Paris, 1968; and P.D. and A.Sen and S.Marglin, *Guidelines for Project Evaluation*, UNIDO, New York, 1972.
12. Little and Mirrless, *op. cit.*, pp.209ff. In the social "Cost-Benefit" analysis, these expenses are put together with what are called "shadow prices". There is no room in this appendix to deal with this process in detail.
13. Max Aebi, "Une fabrique naît à Jamshoro/Kotri (Pakistan)", *Bulletin Sandoz*, no. 24, pp.3ff.
14. H.Bachmann, "Sens et contresens des investissements privés en Amérique latine", *Economie extérieure*, vol. III, 1969, p.235. It is crucial in such a case to consider all the alternative possibilities, and above all to answer the question, "What would have happened if this particular industrial project had never been carried out?"
15. *L'Activité de Nestlé dans les pays en voie de développement*, Vevey, 1973.
16. The brochure gives no details of the amount of milk processed or the production programme.
17. *ILO News*, ILO, no. 1, 1970, p.7.
18. In the case of the above-mentioned Nestlé factory in Mexico, the capital invested amounted to 11,000 francs per job (Nestlé, *op. cit.*, p.27).
19. Gunnar Myrdal, *Manifeste politique*; also *UN Panel on Foreign Investment in Developing Countries*, Amsterdam, 1969, UN/E.69 II. D.12, New York, 1969, p.22.

20. Paul Streeten, "Improving the Climate", *Ceres,* no. 2, Rome, 1969 (PAO), p.56; H.D.Boris, "De l'économie politique des rapports entre sociétés industrielles occidentales", *Argument,* no. 38, Berlin, 1966, p.190; Helmut Arndt, in *Die Zeit,* no. 10, 12 March 1963, p.35; Hans Bachmann, *op. cit.,* pp.236ff.

21. André Guner Frank, *Capitalism and Underdevelopment in Latin America* (Monthly Review Press), 1967.

22. The new double taxation agreement between Switzerland and Trinidad and Tobago could be very harmful to other agreements with other developing countries. By the introduction of a "matching credit", Swiss investors no longer have to make up the difference in Switzerland between the Swiss rate of tax and the lower rate in the developing country. "Message sur un accord de double imposition entre la Suisse et Trinidad / Tobago", *Bundesblatt,* 18 April 1973, no. 20, p.1,228.

23. G.Gorsche, R.Lehmann-Richter, *Les Bénéfices des investissements directs allemands dans les pays en voie de développement* (Bertelsmann), 1970, pp.3, 56, 80.

24. F.Hemmerich, "Le rôle des trusts occidentaux dans le processus économique des pays en voie de développement", *Feuille de politique allemande et internationale,* no. 5, 1971, p.16.

25. Rudolf H. Strahm, *Pays industriels – Pays en voie de développement,* Fribourg and Nüremberg, 1972, pp.94-7.

26. OECD, *Development Assistance,* Paris, 1969, p.255.

27. These figures are not claimed to be exact, but only to reflect the sort of scale on which money flows out of the developing countries.

IV
First Know Your Enemy

9
First Know Your Enemy

At whose table should the Just refuse to sit
If it is to help justice?
What remedy would seem too bitter
For the dying man to swallow?
What infamy would you refuse to commit
To exterminate all infamy?
What would you not agree to,
If it meant you could transform the world?
Who are you?
Wallow in your own filth,
Embrace the hangman, but
Change the world: it needs it!

Bertolt Brecht
"Change the world, it needs it"

We are the pure silver of the earth,
Real human ore.
We are the everlasting sea incarnate –
The fortress of hope.
We are not blinded by a moment's darkness,
And when we die there will be no pain.

Pablo Neruda
"El Episodio", *Memorial de la Isla Negra*

All of us, in varying degrees, are today under attack from the same enemy: the malnutrition, the sickness, the poverty, the hatred and the shame imposed on the many by the few. Imperialism is a cancer. This book is no exhaustive treatise on the subject, but a modest clinical analysis of one specific tumour – auxiliary or "secondary" imperialism. It presents the theoretical and practical knowledge I have acquired during eight years of parliamentary experience, and of activity and discussion among Swiss people. But metastasis will soon occur. The ravages of imperialism are spreading across the globe at a terrifying rate. The only cure is concerted action by men and women determined to put a stop to the monocratic rule of finance capital and of the market place, to get rid of the poverty and the lies, and transform their mutilated lives into a meaningful collective destiny.

In this short conclusion I am not prescribing any political programme: programmes and theories can only grow out of the collective struggle. All I want is to suggest a few lines of thought.

First. The imperialist violence wrought by capitalist society distorts the lives of dependent human beings – into a denatured existence (in

159

the West) or a harsh, unmitigated Calvary (in the Third World). People who are reified and submerged, worn down by fideism and commercial propaganda, are incapable of even recognizing the mechanics of imperialism, let alone of re-structuring their view of the world to take account of it. In the West, therefore, the present phase of the class struggle must be waged with particular force on the theoretical level.

The first, rather obvious-sounding, task of those of the revolutionary left – those, that is, who want to change things – is to preserve a sense of horror. To maintain this sense of horror in one's innermost being, and make it the basis of one's everyday perception of the world, seems to me an indispensable condition for any genuine struggle against imperialism. Our discovery of the crime quietly being perpetrated against so many people must become part of our conscious awareness, and something we formulate in words. What we say must have a single, overriding aim: to show that what is, is false. We must unmask the oligarchies, and use reasoned analysis to disclose the worldwide system of cause and effect upon which their activities are based. The first priority today is to knock down the interpretations they themselves try to make us accept.

Second. How can we destroy intellectually the system of symbols that screens the activities of the primary, secondary and peripheral oligarchies without first physically destroying the repressive systems which ultimately give those symbols their force?

The fundamental problem posed in this book is the problem of the anti-imperialist struggle. How does it relate to the class struggle? Or, more accurately, what is the *international function* of the class struggle today?[1] Let me explain: every class struggle is an anti-imperialist struggle, but not every anti-imperialist struggle is a class struggle. It is a phase of the class struggle, but is not the same thing. For example: the anti-imperialist struggle in Europe today demands unconditional support for OPEC and a rejection of the anti-OPEC policies of the International Energy Agency – even though, from the viewpoint of the class struggle, many of the OPEC leaders are actually class enemies. From the viewpoint of the anti-imperialist struggle, it would be nonsense to denounce Arab emirs for taking control of their national wealth, obliging the multinational oil companies to pay a fair price and freeing their countries from centuries of dependence;[2] on the other hand, it is right and necessary to denounce them as reactionary and anti-popular rulers of their respective states.

To take another example: the "industrial peace" agreed in 1937 in Switzerland represented a betrayal on the part of the working class, and even today they are still not engaged in the struggle as a class. But to reject "industrial peace" does not mean rejecting the alliance of the trade unions with the national bourgeoisie in their struggle against the growing control exercised by the multinational companies over the nation's production system; that could be a successful battle in the war against imperialism, and thus in the class struggle.

A final example: in the class struggle in Europe, it is the fighter's duty to unmask the ideological function of religion in the service of the secondary imperialist oligarchy; but one has an equal duty to support the World Council of Churches in the struggle against apartheid in South Africa.

It seems to me vital to distinguish between the class struggle and the fight against imperialism if we are to ensure that none of our fighters take up positions that are irrelevant or ineffective. No individual can delegate to anyone else the struggle he himself can and must fight wherever he finds himself.

I remember an April night in Geneva in 1964. I had been in Cuba in 1958 and 1959, and I wanted to go back and settle there. My friends in the Cuban delegation to the first Trade Conference had agreed to meet me at the Intercontinental Hotel. We argued till dawn. Among them was Che Guevara, who said to me with that disconcerting friendly irony of his: "But you're right here, in the brain of the monster! What more do you want? This is where you must fight . . ."[3] and he gestured sweepingly over Geneva, just waking up below us, disfigured by its multitude of banks. I was rather hurt by getting such a definite "no" to my proposal to emigrate. But Che was clearly right. Anyone who thinks he can just emigrate, who imagines himself in the role of a Singalese guerrilla, a Palestinian Arab, or a member of the resistance in Chile, is simply surrendering the ground he is standing on to those who now dominate it.[4]

The primary political task of the anti-imperialist struggle involves a wider front than the class struggle as such. Or, to put it another way, the anti-imperialist struggle as a phase of the class struggle demands, in Europe and elsewhere, temporary alliances with the class enemy – though only in so far as such alliances relate to and further the anti-imperialist struggle.[5]

Third. The world can never be reconciled to all the horror and suffering of its past. But this world bears within itself the seeds, the yearnings, the dream that could come true, of a juster, egalitarian society. History carries within it an eschatology. Every human being has a clear awareness of his or her life as something not yet complete. What we can achieve, as a result of the reality we have experienced and the capacities that reality has developed in us, is but the merest fraction of the actions, the feelings, the perceptions of which we are capable in theory.[6] The percentage of unreality – that is to say of what is unrealizable at mankind's present stage of development – in all of us is enormous. It exists in everyone in the shape of a Utopia.

The class struggle and the anti-imperialist struggle ultimately proceed from the same parameters, which are visible in the eschatology of our future development. A worldwide society of solidarity and interdependence, in which active mutual help replaces the profit motive, and an endeavour to find happiness for everyone replaces the present deplorable reason of state (or of class), is today noteworthy by its absence: it exists only in the realm of desire. But that absence is something we are positively aware of, and desire is a force of History.

It would take a far longer book than this for me to recall the function of hope and Utopian ideas in the revolutionary process. What I want to say is best summed up in a Venezuelan peasant song:[7]

> *Se puede matar el hombre*
> *Pero no matarán la forma*
> *En que se alegraba su alma*
> *Cuando soñaba ser libre.* *

---

* Man may be killed, but they will never kill the happiness he feels when he dreams of being free.

1. At this point it is helpful to go back to Marx. He wrote a violent critique of the programme of the German workers' party, known as the Gotha programme. In that programme, the attack on imperialism was treated at a purely subjective level: the class struggle was supposed to give German revolutionaries a consciousness of "the international brotherhood of peoples". But it is not just a psychological conversion that is needed, not just good intentions. There is an instrumental material link between the class struggle and the struggle against imperialism. In this sense, I will never put the same interpretation on the historical function of the anti-imperialist struggle as do my bourgeois colleagues.
2. This is true even though the actions of OPEC are having a disastrous effect on Third World countries that are not oil producers; they support OPEC in spite of that fact.
3. I have described this interview in a symposium entitled, *Guevara, ein Revolutionär*, Frankfurt am Main (Fischer), 1969, p.68ff.
4. One cannot, however, deduce from this that the coming to power of a Left coalition in France or Switzerland would suddenly change the conditions of exploitation and domination in which the Third World lives vis-à-vis the countries of the centre (though of course it must mark an important stage in the class struggle at home). For instance, it would mean dismantling an enormous armaments industry geared to export, causing such a loss of jobs as would be quite impossible to sustain, or to make up in the immediate future. On the other hand, if every European eats 50 kilos of meat per year, whereas those in the Third World have under 5 kilos, and the amount a person strictly needs is 20 kilos per year, then a worldwide equalization of food purchasing power would demand a great reduction in the standard of living of everyone in the West. Such a worldwide redistribution would be a necessary pre-condition for the setting up of any world political system – and is clearly not being considered by any of the present-day parties of the Left in Europe.
We may note finally that the same thing works the other way on the periphery. Several Third World countries – China, Cuba, Algeria, for instance – have achieved impressive changes in terms of internal revolution and the construction of an equitable society within their borders. But for obvious reasons none of these can have a purely anti-imperialist military and commercial foreign policy. To survive, they all make certain concessions to the world imperialist system: they can only fight their enemies one at a time.
5. The problem of humanitarian aid, technological co-operation, the Red Cross, and so on, is different in kind: it does not fall within the terms of the anti-imperialist struggle, nor has it any bearing on alliances. Anti-imperialists are divided about it: there is no doubt that most humanitarian institutions serve as alibis for the oligarchy, helping to disguise the evil they have already done. But I do not believe one should rigidly refuse to collaborate with them. I should say that what we are dealing with is human life, and that if humanitarian aid from a capitalist state or a charitable organization financed by private gifts (some of them from the oligarchy) makes it possible to save the life of a single child, it should be supported. If the International Committee of Red Cross can get a single victim out of the camps of Santiago, the gaols of Paraguay or Czechoslovakia, then it deserves our support, even though its members include directors of multi-national companies (Ciba-Geigy, Nestlé, the Fédération horlogère). No idea should prevail against a life; or, more precisely, the survival of a child

or the saving of a prisoner are not in the realm of ideas.

6. When I say "in theory", I use the word in its etymological sense: a mental vision, a total vision, the vision of the unifying principle of God; cf. E.Bloch, *Prinzip Hoffnung,* vol. II, 1959.

7. From *Vas caminando sin huellas* . . . , Vienna (Plaène), 1974.

Postscript

This book was published on 2 April 1976. I write this epilogue a year and a half later.

Over 160,000 copies have been sold, and fifteen foreign editions are either published or in preparation. Hundreds of letters and dozen of discussions have introduced me to an unsuspected world of human brotherhood, and disclosed the existence of that invisible party of the revolution that is the leaven of our time and the hope of the world.

In Switzerland, where a supposedly "factual" national press[1] stirred up the most painful anxieties in my compatriots, my life has changed: threats to my family and myself have obliged me to seek police protection from time to time, and to be on my guard at all times.

Why has this book had such an effect? Perhaps because its publication coincided in France and in Spain with the advance towards political power of coalitions of progressive forces offering programmes for a new society. That embodiment of human hope in a powerful and visible social movement further coincided with a patent crisis in the ideology, the political hierarchy and the method of government of monopolistic capitalism. Suddenly new ideas – or old ideas rescued from long oblivion – were being entertained and debated by the collective consciousness: people were suddenly noticing the symbolic violence of finance capital, the ravages it causes in the societies of the Third World, the system of international economic sabotage effected by the deliberate withdrawal of capital from industries and its removal from the country (as in Chile in 1972).

As though to confirm some of the points my book makes, the past year has provided a wealth of examples: I will content myself with citing the case of the Crédit Suisse scandal.[2] What happened was this: the Chiasso[3] branch of the Crédit Suisse was told to get all its capital out of Italy (it was feared that the Communists were about to come to power); the money was transported – secretly and illegally – to Chiasso, whence it was transferred to Liechtenstein to fictitious companies which "laundered" the money and then invested it perfectly legally in various enterprises in Italy (a luxury tourist centre on the Adriatic, for instance). This operation involved sums amounting to the equivalent of 2.2 billion Swiss francs owned by some 1,000 Italian investors. The clients lost about 1.4 billion in the process, but the Crédit Suisse is an "honest" dealer, and declared its intention of repaying its customers.[4]

To confound the investigations of European tax authorities, Swiss banks have to convert illegal funds into a succession of different currencies – whose exchange rate cannot always be known in advance. The bankers in the Paradeplatz in Zürich are among the best in the world. Their failure presents capitalists the world over with a totally new problem: a choice between losing their capital, sending it to Switzerland despite the risks, or collaborating with the future left-wing governments of their countries. The mere fact that this problem must henceforth be reckoned with constitutes – especially in France and Italy – an unparalleled opportunity for a peaceful, democratic transition towards a socialist economy of self-management.

Knowledge, to be effective, must be initiatory knowledge, a knowledge born out of collective action. Capitalist market society, the graves it fills day by day in the dependent countries, the symbolic violence whereby it maintains its power at the centre – none of these will be destroyed by words. But a book *can* help those who are dominated to become aware of their own strength, and to see that "what is, is false". Colombian children do not come to die in the Bahnhofstrasse in Zürich or the rue de la Corraterie in Geneva. The worthy bankers, brokers, speculators and money-men of all kinds who arrive at their air-conditioned offices every morning, the fortresses of their multinational finance domination, do not stumble over the shattered, skeletal bodies of Brazilian beggars on the pavement.

As I write – freely – tens of thousands of men, women and children are being killed, starved or tortured to death in countries in Latin America, Africa and Asia where the multinational companies and their puppets reign supreme (Pinochet, Videla, Marcos, Mobutu). The first credit for aid to go to the hangmen of Buenos Aires came from Switzerland: 300 million dollars, in December 1976. In April 1977, the Bührle-Oerlikon group set up in Brazil the biggest armaments works in the whole of Latin America.

Swiss bankers kill without machine-guns or napalm or troops. No man is an island. Every human being, and therefore every nation, subsists only with the help of others, in reciprocity and mutual fulfilment. There can be no real happiness for any of us until every human being – whether in Argentina or Cambodia, in Chile, Indonesia or Brazil – is free. By demonstrating the ways in which death is caused, by denouncing the mechanisms which condemn thousands of people far away from us to subhuman lives – via our telex and our stock-exchange and their local dictatorships – I want also to contribute to the liberation of the Swiss people.

We all have the sense that an epoch in human history is coming to an end. The bourgeois ideology, the ideology of the sham consensus, of a hierarchy of power, of statutory inequality among individuals and nations, the crazy ideology of collaboration between share capital and the labour of exploited human beings, is nearly over and done with. It no longer convinces anyone. For so long, we – socialists, revolutionaries – have been night-watchmen, the ancestors, if you like, of the future. Now we can say – with the libertarians of the Jura in the time of the First International – "the truce and the lying are over. Peace to mankind – but war to the capitalist system!"

Jean Ziegler
November 1977

Notes to Postscript

1. When this book appeared, the Swiss press – i.e. the major Swiss papers such as the *Neue Zürcher Zeitung, Tribune de Genève, Journal de Genève* – took upon itself a twofold mission: to evade all public debate on the points raised in it, and to "pathologize" its author. Then, later on (spring 1977), the oligarchy changed their tactics. They got two books published to refute me: *Une Suisse insoupconnée* (Buchet-Chastel) was written by Victor Lasserre, editor of *L'Ordre professionnel,* the official organ of the employers' associations in Geneva; and *Des professeurs répondent à Jean Ziegler,* published by the public relations department of the Vorort, and written by Professors Gruner, Schaller and Kleinewerfers.

2. *Le Monde* carried a front-page headline: "The Crédit Suisse scandal is the worst in Swiss History" (April 1977). I do not agree: the Crédit Suisse scandal is merely one instance of the usual banditry of the banks. The only unusual thing is that the law caught up with it.

3. A frontier town in Ticino – a canton with 267,000 inhabitants and 1,437 banks and finance companies.

4. The profits of the Crédit Suisse rose by 16 per cent in 1975, totalling over 40 billion Swiss francs.

Index of Names